Home Sweet Home COOKBOOK

Publications International, Ltd.

Photograph on front cover and page 170 © Shutterstock.com. All other photographs copyright © Publications International, Ltd.

Pictured on the front cover: Classic Apple Pie *(page 170)*.

Pictured on the back cover *(clockwise from top left):* Sawmill Biscuits and Gravy *(page 14)*, Sausage Rice Soup *(page 48)*, Broccoli and Cauliflower Salad *(page 145)* and Simple Roasted Chicken *(page 85)*.

ISBN: 978-1-64558-563-3

Manufactured in China.

8 7 6 5 4 3 2 1

Microwave Cooking: Microwave ovens vary in wattage. Use the cooking times as guidelines and check for doneness before adding more time.

Let's get social!
@Publications_International
@PublicationsInternational
www.pilbooks.com

CONTENTS

BREAKFAST

STRAWBERRY BANANA FRENCH TOAST

MAKES 2 SERVINGS

1 cup sliced fresh strawberries (about 8 medium)

2 teaspoons sugar

2 eggs

½ cup milk

3 tablespoons all-purpose flour

1 teaspoon vanilla

⅛ teaspoon salt

1 tablespoon butter

4 slices (1 inch thick) egg bread or country bread

1 banana, cut into ¼-inch slices

Whipped cream and powdered sugar (optional)

Maple syrup

1. Combine strawberries and sugar in small bowl; toss to coat. Set aside while preparing French toast.

2. Whisk eggs, milk, flour, vanilla and salt in shallow bowl or pie plate until well blended. Melt ½ tablespoon butter in large skillet over medium-high heat. Working with 2 slices at a time, dip bread into egg mixture, turning to coat completely; let excess drip off. Add to skillet; cook 3 to 4 minutes per side or until golden brown. Repeat with remaining butter and bread slices.

3. Top each serving with strawberry mixture and banana slices. Garnish with whipped cream and powdered sugar; serve with maple syrup.

ZUCCHINI-TOMATO FRITTATA

MAKES 4 SERVINGS

1 cup sliced zucchini

1 cup broccoli florets

1 cup diced red or yellow bell pepper

6 eggs

½ cup cottage cheese

½ cup rehydrated* sun-dried tomatoes (1 ounce dry), coarsely chopped

¼ cup chopped green onions

¼ cup chopped fresh basil

⅛ teaspoon ground red pepper

2 tablespoons grated Parmesan cheese

Paprika

*To rehydrate sun-dried tomatoes, pour 1 cup boiling water over tomatoes in small bowl. Let soak 5 to 10 minutes or until softened; drain well.

1. Preheat broiler. Spray 10-inch ovenproof skillet with nonstick cooking spray; heat over medium-high heat. Add zucchini, broccoli and bell pepper; cook and stir 3 to 4 minutes or until vegetables are crisp-tender.

2. Whisk eggs, cottage cheese, tomatoes, green onions, basil and ground red pepper in medium bowl until well blended. Pour egg mixture over vegetables in skillet. Cook, uncovered, gently lifting sides of frittata so uncooked egg flows underneath. Cook 7 to 8 minutes or until frittata is almost firm and golden brown on bottom. Remove from heat; sprinkle with Parmesan cheese.

3. Broil about 5 inches from heat 3 to 5 minutes or until golden brown. Sprinkle with paprika. Cut into four wedges. Serve immediately.

BAKED APPLE PANCAKE

MAKES 2 TO 4 SERVINGS

- 3 tablespoons butter
- 3 medium Granny Smith apples (about 1¼ pounds), peeled and cut into ¼-inch slices
- ½ cup packed dark brown sugar
- 1½ teaspoons ground cinnamon
- ½ teaspoon plus pinch of salt, divided
- 4 eggs
- ⅓ cup whipping cream
- ⅓ cup milk
- 2 tablespoons granulated sugar
- ½ teaspoon vanilla
- ⅔ cup all-purpose flour

1. Melt butter in 8-inch ovenproof nonstick or cast iron skillet over medium heat. Add apples, brown sugar, cinnamon and pinch of salt; cook 8 minutes or until apples begin to soften, stirring occasionally. Spread apples in even layer in skillet; set aside to cool 30 minutes.

2. After apples have cooled 30 minutes, preheat oven to 425°F. Whisk eggs in large bowl until foamy. Add cream, milk, granulated sugar, vanilla and remaining ½ teaspoon salt; whisk until blended. Sift flour into egg mixture; whisk until batter is well blended and smooth. Set aside 15 minutes.

3. Stir batter; pour evenly over apple mixture. Place skillet on rimmed baking sheet in case of drips (or place baking sheet or piece of foil in oven beneath skillet).

4. Bake 16 minutes or until top is golden brown and pancake is loose around edge. Cool 1 minute; loosen edge of pancake with spatula, if necessary. Place large serving plate or cutting board on top of skillet and invert pancake onto plate. Serve warm.

CHORIZO-POTATO HASH WITH CRISP CRUMB TOPPING

MAKES 6 SERVINGS

1 naan bread, torn into uneven pieces

6 tablespoons plus 1 teaspoon olive oil, divided

Kosher salt and black pepper

1 pound Mexican chorizo, casings removed

1 onion, diced

1 yellow bell pepper, diced

1 red bell pepper, diced

2 Russet potatoes, peeled, shredded, rinsed and squeezed dry *or* 1 bag (1 pound 4 ounces) refrigerated shredded hash brown potatoes

1 green onion, sliced on the bias

1. Place naan pieces in food processor; pulse until small crumbs form, about 15 pulses. Transfer to large bowl; toss with 2 tablespoons oil.

2. Heat large cast iron skillet over medium heat. Add crumbs; cook 6 to 8 minutes or until browned and toasted, stirring occasionally. Season with salt and black pepper; set aside.

3. Heat 1 teaspoon oil in same skillet over medium-high heat. Add chorizo; cook 5 minutes or until browned, using spatula to break up the meat. Transfer to paper towel-lined plate. Heat 1 tablespoon oil in same skillet; add onion and bell peppers; cook 8 minutes or until tender, stirring occasionally. Season with salt and black pepper. Transfer to bowl.

4. Heat remaining 3 tablespoons oil in same skillet; add potatoes in even layer; cook 3 minutes or until browned and beginning to crisp on bottom. Turn potatoes, continue to cook 10 minutes or until tender and evenly browned, stirring occasionally. Season with salt and black pepper. Stir in chorizo and onion-bell pepper mixture; cook 2 minutes or until heated through. Top with bread crumbs and green onion.

TIP: This recipe is especially good to make when you have day-old or stale naan bread.

BAKED PUMPKIN OATMEAL

MAKES 6 SERVINGS

- 2 **cups old-fashioned oats**
- 2 **cups milk**
- 1 **cup canned pumpkin**
- 2 **eggs**
- ⅓ **cup packed brown sugar**
- 1 **teaspoon vanilla**
- ½ **cup dried cranberries, plus additional for topping**
- 1 **teaspoon pumpkin pie spice**
- ½ **teaspoon salt**
- ½ **teaspoon baking powder**
- **Maple syrup**
- **Chopped pecans (optional)**

1. Preheat oven to 350°F. Spray 8-inch square baking dish with nonstick cooking spray.

2. Spread oats on ungreased baking sheet. Bake 10 minutes or until fragrant and lightly browned, stirring occasionally. Pour into medium bowl; let cool slightly.

3. Whisk milk, pumpkin, eggs, brown sugar and vanilla in large bowl until well blended. Add ½ cup cranberries, pumpkin pie spice, salt and baking powder to oats; mix well. Add oat mixture to pumpkin mixture; stir until well blended. Pour into prepared baking dish.

4. Bake 45 minutes or until set and knife inserted into center comes out almost clean. Serve warm with maple syrup, additional cranberries and pecans, if desired.

SAWMILL BISCUITS AND GRAVY

MAKES 8 SERVINGS

3 tablespoons canola or vegetable oil, divided

8 ounces bulk breakfast sausage

2¼ cups plus 3 tablespoons biscuit baking mix, divided

2⅔ cups whole milk, divided

¼ teaspoon salt

¼ teaspoon black pepper

Fresh fruit (optional)

1. Preheat oven to 450°F. Heat 1 tablespoon oil in large skillet over medium heat. Add sausage; cook and stir 6 to 8 minutes or until browned, stirring to break up meat. Remove to plate using slotted spoon.

2. Add remaining 2 tablespoons oil to skillet. Add 3 tablespoons biscuit mix; whisk until smooth. Gradually add 2 cups milk; cook and stir 3 to 4 minutes or until mixture comes to a boil. Cook and stir 1 minute or until thickened. Add sausage and any juices; cook and stir 2 minutes. Season with salt and pepper.

3. Combine remaining 2¼ cups biscuit mix and ⅔ cup milk in medium bowl; stir until blended. Spoon batter into eight mounds onto gravy mixture.

4. Bake 8 to 10 minutes or until golden. Serve warm with gravy. Serve with fruit, if desired.

BACON & POTATO FRITTATA

MAKES 4 TO 6 SERVINGS

5 **eggs**

½ **cup bacon, crisp-cooked and crumbled**

¼ **cup half-and-half or milk**

⅛ **teaspoon salt**

⅛ **teaspoon black pepper**

3 **tablespoons butter**

2 **cups frozen O'Brien hash brown potatoes with onions and peppers**

1. Preheat broiler. Beat eggs in medium bowl. Add bacon, half-and-half, salt and pepper; beat until well blended.

2. Melt butter in large ovenproof skillet over medium-high heat. Add potatoes; cook and stir 4 minutes. Pour egg mixture into skillet. Reduce heat to medium; cover and cook 6 minutes or until eggs are set at edges (top will still be wet).

3. Transfer skillet to broiler. Broil 4 inches from heat source 1 to 2 minutes or until top is golden brown and center is set.

SERVING SUGGESTION: Top frittata with red bell pepper strips, chopped fresh chives and salsa.

MAPLE PECAN GRANOLA

MAKES ABOUT 6 CUPS

6 tablespoons vegetable oil

¼ cup maple syrup, plus additional for serving

¼ cup packed dark brown sugar

1½ teaspoons vanilla

½ teaspoon coarse salt

½ teaspoon ground cinnamon

3 cups old-fashioned rolled oats

1½ cups pecans, coarsely chopped

¾ cup shredded coconut

¼ cup ground flaxseed

¼ cup water

Plain yogurt or milk (optional)

1. Preheat oven to 350°F. Line baking sheet with parchment paper.

2. Whisk oil, ¼ cup maple syrup, brown sugar, vanilla, salt and cinnamon in large bowl until blended. Stir in oats, pecans, coconut and flaxseed until evenly coated. Stir in water. Spread mixture on prepared baking sheet, pressing into even layer.

3. Bake 30 minutes or until golden brown and fragrant. Cool completely on baking sheet. Serve with yogurt and additional maple syrup, if desired. Store leftovers in an airtight container at room temperature 1 month.

NOTE: For chunky granola, do not stir during baking. For loose granola, stir every 10 minutes during baking.

FRENCH TOAST STRATA

MAKES 6 SERVINGS

4 cups (4 ounces) day-old French or Italian bread, cut into large cubes

⅓ cup golden raisins

3 ounces cream cheese, cut into ¼-inch cubes

3 eggs

1½ cups milk

½ cup maple syrup, plus additional for serving

1 teaspoon vanilla

2 tablespoons sugar

1 teaspoon ground cinnamon

1. Spray 11×7-inch baking dish with nonstick cooking spray. Place bread cubes in even layer in dish; sprinkle raisins and cream cheese evenly over bread.

2. Beat eggs in medium bowl. Add milk, ½ cup maple syrup and vanilla; beat until well blended. Pour egg mixture over bread mixture; cover and refrigerate at least 4 hours or overnight.

3. Preheat oven to 350°F. Combine sugar and cinnamon in small bowl; sprinkle over strata.

4. Bake, uncovered, 40 to 45 minutes or until puffed, golden brown and knife inserted into center comes out clean. Serve warm with additional maple syrup.

SERVING SUGGESTION: Serve with mixed fresh fruit.

HAM & SWISS CHEESE BISCUITS

MAKES ABOUT 18 BISCUITS

2 cups all-purpose flour

2 teaspoons baking powder

½ teaspoon baking soda

½ cup (1 stick) butter, cut into small pieces

⅔ cup buttermilk

½ cup (2 ounces) shredded Swiss cheese

2 ounces ham, minced

1. Preheat oven to 450°F. Grease baking sheet.

2. Combine flour, baking powder and baking soda in medium bowl. Cut in butter with pastry blender or two knives until mixture resembles coarse crumbs. Stir in buttermilk, 1 tablespoon at a time, until slightly sticky dough forms. Stir in cheese and ham.

3. Turn out dough onto lightly floured surface; knead lightly. Roll out dough to ½-inch thickness. Cut out biscuits with 2-inch round cutter. Place on prepared baking sheet.

4. Bake 10 minutes or until browned. Serve warm.

SNACKS

PARMESAN RANCH SNACK MIX

MAKES ABOUT 9½ CUPS

3 cups corn or rice cereal squares

2 cups oyster crackers

1 package (5 ounces) bagel chips, broken in half

1½ cups mini pretzel twists

1 cup shelled pistachio nuts

2 tablespoons grated Parmesan cheese

¼ cup (½ stick) butter, melted

1 package (1 ounce) dry ranch salad dressing mix

½ teaspoon garlic powder

SLOW COOKER DIRECTIONS

1. Combine cereal, oyster crackers, bagel chips, pretzels, pistachios and cheese in slow cooker; toss gently.

2. Combine butter, salad dressing mix and garlic powder in small bowl. Pour over cereal mixture; toss lightly to coat. Cover; cook on LOW 3 hours.

3. Remove cover; stir gently. Cook, uncovered, on LOW 30 minutes.

TAMALE PIE DIP

MAKES ABOUT 5 CUPS

1 package (8 ounces) cream cheese

2 cups (8 ounces) shredded Mexican-style cheese, divided

1 can (8 ounces) creamed corn

1 can (8 ounces) diced tomatoes

½ cup sour cream

2 cloves garlic, minced

1 teaspoon chili powder

2 cups diced cooked chicken

1 teaspoon olive oil

Optional toppings: sour cream, sliced or chopped black olives, diced avocado, sliced green onions and/or diced tomato

Tortilla chips

1. Preheat oven to 325°F. Coat 9-inch quiche dish or deep-dish pie plate with nonstick cooking spray; set aside.

2. Process cream cheese, 1 cup Mexican-style cheese, corn, tomatoes, sour cream, garlic and chili powder in food processor or blender until almost smooth. Stir in chicken by hand. Spoon mixture into prepared dish. Top with remaining 1 cup Mexican-style cheese. Drizzle with oil. Bake 45 minutes.

3. Garnish as desired. Serve with tortilla chips.

CHEESY GARLIC BREAD

MAKES 8 TO 10 SERVINGS

1 loaf (about 16 ounces) Italian bread

½ cup (1 stick) butter, softened

8 cloves garlic, very thinly sliced

¼ cup grated Parmesan cheese

2 cups (8 ounces) shredded mozzarella cheese

1. Preheat oven to 425°F. Line large baking sheet with foil.

2. Cut bread in half horizontally. Spread cut sides of bread evenly with butter; top with sliced garlic. Sprinkle with Parmesan cheese, then mozzarella cheese. Place on prepared baking sheet.

3. Bake 12 minutes or until cheeses are melted and golden brown in spots. Cut crosswise into slices. Serve warm.

28

CRISPY RANCH CHICKEN BITES

7-LAYER DIP

MAKES 10 SERVINGS

1 package (3 ounces) ramen noodles, any flavor, crushed*

2 tablespoons taco seasoning mix

3 ripe avocados, diced

1 jalapeño pepper, finely chopped

2 tablespoons finely chopped fresh cilantro

2 tablespoons lime juice

1 clove garlic, minced

½ teaspoon salt

1 can (about 15 ounces) refried beans

1 container (16 ounces) sour cream

2 cups (8 ounces) shredded Mexican Cheddar–Jack cheese

2 medium tomatoes, diced

3 green onions, thinly sliced

Tortilla chips

*Discard seasoning packet.

1. Combine noodles and taco seasoning mix in medium bowl; mix well.

2. Mash avocados, jalapeño, cilantro, lime juice, garlic and salt in large bowl.

3. Spread refried beans in bottom of 8-inch glass baking dish. Layer sour cream, noodles, avocado mixture, cheese, tomatoes and green onions evenly over beans. Serve immediately or cover and refrigerate for up to 8 hours. Serve with tortilla chips.

PARMESAN PICKLE CHIPS

MAKES 4 SERVINGS

4 large whole dill pickles

1 egg

½ cup panko bread crumbs

2 tablespoons grated Parmesan cheese

Salt and black pepper

½ cup garlic aioli mayonnaise or ranch dressing

1. Slice pickles diagonally into ¼-inch slices. Pat dry with paper towels to remove any moisture from pickles.

2. Beat egg in shallow dish. Combine panko and cheese in another shallow dish.

3. Dip pickle slices in egg, letting excess drip off, then coat in panko mixture. Place on baking sheet; sprinkle with salt and pepper.

4. Preheat oven to 450°F. Bake 12 to 14 minutes or until golden brown. Remove carefully. Serve with aioli.

SPICY BAKED SWEET POTATO CHIPS

MAKES 4 SERVINGS

1 teaspoon sugar

½ teaspoon smoked paprika

¼ teaspoon salt

¼ teaspoon ground red pepper

2 medium sweet potatoes, unpeeled

1 tablespoon plus 1 teaspoon vegetable oil

1. Preheat oven to 400°F. Spray baking sheet with nonstick cooking spray. Combine sugar, paprika, salt and ground red pepper in small bowl; set aside.

2. Cut sweet potatoes crosswise into very thin slices, about ⅟₁₆ inch thick. Place on prepared baking sheet. Drizzle with oil; toss to coat. Arrange in single layer.

3. Bake 10 minutes. Turn chips over; sprinkle with seasoning mix. Bake 10 to 15 minutes or until chips are lightly browned and crisp, stirring frequently. Spread on paper towels to cool completely.

PARMESAN PICKLE CHIPS

GARLIC-PARMESAN POPCORN

MAKES 12 CUPS POPCORN

1 tablespoon olive oil

1 clove garlic, finely minced

1 tablespoon light butter-and-oil spread, melted

12 cups plain popped popcorn

⅓ cup finely grated Parmesan cheese

½ teaspoon dried basil

½ teaspoon dried oregano

Stir oil and garlic into spread in small bowl until well blended. Pour over popcorn in large bowl; toss to coat. Sprinkle with cheese, basil and oregano.

TIP: One regular-size microwavable package of popcorn yields about 10 to 12 cups of popped popcorn.

SWEET & SPICY POPCORN CLUSTERS

MAKES 6 SERVINGS

½ cup sugar

6 tablespoons (¾ stick) butter

4 teaspoons light corn syrup

½ teaspoon salt

½ teaspoon ground red pepper

12 cups popped butter-flavored microwave popcorn

1. Combine sugar, butter, corn syrup, salt and ground red pepper in large saucepan. Bring to a boil over medium heat; boil 3 minutes. Remove from heat.

2. Immediately stir in popcorn; toss to coat evenly.

3. Spread mixture in single layer on baking sheets. Let stand 1 hour to cool completely. Break into clusters. Store in airtight container.

GARLIC-PARMESAN POPCORN

PEPPERONI PIZZA ROLLS

MAKES 12 ROLLS

1 loaf (16 ounces) frozen pizza dough or white bread dough, thawed according to package directions

½ cup pizza sauce, plus additional sauce for serving

⅓ cup chopped pepperoni or mini pepperoni slices (half of 2½-ounce package)

9 to 10 slices (1 ounce each) fontina, provolone or provolone-mozzarella blend cheese*

*For best results, use thinner cheese slices which are less than 1 ounce each.

1. Spray 12 standard (2½-inch) muffin pan cups with nonstick cooking spray.

2. Roll out dough on lightly floured surface into 12×10-inch rectangle. Spread ½ cup pizza sauce over dough, leaving ½-inch border on one long side. Sprinkle with pepperoni; top with cheese, cutting slices to fit as necessary. Starting with long side opposite ½-inch border, tightly roll up dough; pinch seam to seal.

3. Cut crosswise into 1-inch slices; place slices cut sides up in prepared muffin cups. Cover with plastic wrap; let rise in warm place 30 to 40 minutes or until nearly doubled in size. Preheat oven to 350°F.

4. Bake 25 minutes or until golden brown. Loosen bottom and sides with small spatula or knife; remove to wire rack. Serve warm with additional sauce for dipping, if desired.

CHICKEN BACON QUESADILLAS

MAKES 4 SERVINGS

4 teaspoons vegetable oil, divided

4 (8-inch) flour tortillas

1 cup (4 ounces) shredded Colby-Jack cheese

2 cups coarsely chopped cooked chicken

4 slices bacon, crisp-cooked and coarsely chopped

½ cup pico de gallo, plus additional for serving

Sour cream and guacamole (optional)

1. Heat large nonstick skillet over medium heat; brush with 1 teaspoon oil. Place one tortilla in skillet; sprinkle with ¼ cup cheese. Spread ½ cup chicken over one half of tortilla; top with one fourth of bacon and 2 tablespoons pico de gallo.

2. Cook 1 to 2 minutes or until cheese is melted and bottom of tortilla is lightly browned. Fold tortilla over filling, pressing with spatula. Transfer to large cutting board; cool slightly. Cut into wedges. Repeat with remaining ingredients. Serve with additional pico de gallo, sour cream and guacamole, if desired.

SOFT PRETZEL BITES WITH CREAMY HONEY MUSTARD

MAKES 12 SERVINGS

¾ **cup sour cream**

¼ **cup Dijon mustard**

3 **tablespoons honey**

1⅔ **cups warm water (110° to 115°F)**

1 **package (¼ ounce) active dry yeast**

2 **teaspoons sugar**

½ **teaspoon table salt**

4½ **cups all-purpose flour, plus additional for work surface**

2 **tablespoons unsalted butter, softened**

12 **cups water**

½ **cup baking soda**

Kosher salt (optional)

1. For creamy honey mustard, stir sour cream, mustard and honey in small bowl until smooth and well blended. Cover; refrigerate until ready to use.

2. Whisk 1⅔ cups warm water, yeast, sugar and table salt in large bowl. Let stand 5 minutes or until bubbly.

3. Add 4½ cups flour and butter to yeast mixture; beat with electric mixer at low speed until combined, scraping sides of bowl occasionally. Replace paddle attachment with dough hook. Beat at medium speed 5 minutes. (If dough wraps around hook, remove and place at bottom of bowl and resume.)

4. Place dough in large bowl sprayed with nonstick cooking spray; turn to coat top. Cover; let rise in warm place 1 hour or until doubled in size.

5. Preheat oven to 450°F. Line baking sheets with foil; spray with cooking spray.

6. Punch down dough; transfer to floured work surface. Flatten and stretch dough into 12 equal pieces. Roll each piece into 12-inch-long rope. Cut each rope into eight equal pieces.

7. Bring 12 cups water to a boil in large saucepan. Stir in baking soda until dissolved. Working in batches, drop dough pieces into boiling water; boil 30 seconds. Remove to prepared baking sheets using slotted spoon.

8. Sprinkle pieces evenly with kosher salt, if desired. Bake 12 minutes or until dark golden brown, rotating baking sheets halfway through. Serve with creamy honey mustard.

SOUPS

TORTILLA SOUP

MAKES 4 SERVINGS

Vegetable oil

3 (6- or 7-inch) corn tortillas, halved and cut into strips

½ cup chopped onion

1 clove garlic, minced

2 cans (about 14 ounces each) chicken broth

1 can (about 14 ounces) diced tomatoes

1 cup shredded cooked chicken

2 teaspoons fresh lime juice

1 small avocado, diced

2 tablespoons chopped fresh cilantro

1. Pour oil to depth of ½ inch in small skillet. Heat over medium-high heat until oil reaches 360°F on deep-fry thermometer. Add tortilla strips, a few at a time; fry 1 minute or until crisp and lightly browned. Remove with slotted spoon; drain on paper towels.

2. Heat 2 teaspoons oil in large saucepan over medium heat. Add onion and garlic; cook and stir 6 to 8 minutes or until onion is softened. Add broth and tomatoes; bring to a boil. Cover; reduce heat to low. Simmer 15 minutes.

3. Add chicken and lime juice; simmer 5 minutes. Top soup with tortilla strips, avocado and cilantro.

CHICKEN ENCHILADA SOUP

MAKES 8 TO 10 SERVINGS

2 tablespoons vegetable oil, divided

1½ pounds boneless skinless chicken breasts, cut into ½-inch pieces

½ cup chopped onion

2 cloves garlic, minced

2 cans (about 14 ounces each) chicken broth

3 cups water, divided

1 cup masa harina

1 package (16 ounces) pasteurized process cheese product, cubed

1 can (10 ounces) mild red enchilada sauce

1 teaspoon chili powder

½ teaspoon salt

½ teaspoon ground cumin

1 large tomato, seeded and chopped

Crispy tortilla strips*

*If tortilla strips are not available, crumble tortilla chips into bite-size pieces.

1. Heat 1 tablespoon oil in large saucepan or Dutch oven over medium-high heat. Add chicken; cook and stir 10 minutes or until no longer pink. Transfer to medium bowl with slotted spoon; drain excess liquid from saucepan.

2. Heat remaining 1 tablespoon oil in same saucepan over medium-high heat. Add onion and garlic; cook and stir 3 minutes or until softened. Stir in broth.

3. Whisk 2 cups water into masa harina in large bowl until smooth. Whisk mixture into broth in saucepan. Stir in remaining 1 cup water, cheese product, enchilada sauce, chili powder, salt and cumin; bring to a boil over high heat. Add chicken. Reduce heat to medium-low. Simmer 30 minutes, stirring frequently. Ladle soup into bowls; top with tomato and tortilla strips.

SAUSAGE RICE SOUP

MAKES 4 TO 6 SERVINGS

2 teaspoons olive oil

8 ounces Italian sausage, casings removed

1 small onion, chopped

½ teaspoon fennel seeds

1 tablespoon tomato paste

4 cups chicken broth

1 can (about 14 ounces) whole tomatoes, undrained, tomatoes crushed with hands or chopped

1½ cups water

½ cup uncooked rice

¼ teaspoon salt

⅛ teaspoon black pepper

2 to 3 ounces baby spinach

⅓ cup shredded mozzarella cheese (optional)

1. Heat oil in large saucepan or Dutch oven over medium-high heat. Add sausage; cook 8 minutes or until browned, stirring to break up meat. Add onion; cook and stir 5 minutes or until softened. Add fennel seeds; cook and stir 30 seconds. Add tomato paste; cook and stir 1 minute.

2. Stir in broth, tomatoes with juice, water, rice, ¼ teaspoon salt and ⅛ teaspoon pepper; bring to a boil. Reduce heat to medium-low. Cook 18 minutes or until rice is tender. Stir in spinach; cook 3 minutes or until wilted. Season with additional salt and pepper.

3. Sprinkle with cheese, if desired, just before serving.

BEEF VEGETABLE SOUP

MAKES 6 TO 8 SERVINGS

1½ **pounds cubed beef stew meat**

¼ **cup all-purpose flour**

3 **tablespoons vegetable oil, divided**

1 **onion, chopped**

2 **stalks celery, chopped**

3 **tablespoons tomato paste**

2 **teaspoons salt**

1 **teaspoon dried thyme**

½ **teaspoon garlic powder**

¼ **teaspoon black pepper**

6 **cups beef broth, divided**

1 **can (28 ounces) stewed tomatoes, undrained**

1 **tablespoon Worcestershire sauce**

1 **bay leaf**

4 **unpeeled red potatoes (about 1 pound), cut into 1-inch pieces**

3 **medium carrots, cut in half lengthwise and cut into ½-inch slices**

6 **ounces green beans, trimmed and cut into 1-inch pieces**

1 **cup frozen corn**

1. Combine beef and flour in medium bowl; toss to coat. Heat 1 tablespoon oil in large saucepan or Dutch oven over medium-high heat. Cook beef in two batches 5 minutes or until browned on all sides, adding additional 1 tablespoon oil after first batch. Remove beef to medium bowl.

2. Heat remaining 1 tablespoon oil in same saucepan. Add onion and celery; cook and stir 5 minutes or until softened. Add tomato paste, 2 teaspoons salt, thyme, garlic powder and ¼ teaspoon pepper; cook and stir 1 minute. Stir in 1 cup broth, scraping up browned bits from bottom of saucepan. Stir in remaining 5 cups broth, tomatoes with juice, Worcestershire sauce, bay leaf and beef; bring to a boil.

3. Reduce heat to low; cover and simmer 1 hour and 20 minutes. Add potatoes and carrots; cook 15 minutes. Add green beans and corn; cook 15 minutes or until vegetables are tender. Remove and discard bay leaf. Season with additional salt and pepper.

CREAMY ONION SOUP

MAKES 4 SERVINGS

6 tablespoons (¾ stick) butter, divided

1 large sweet onion, thinly sliced (about 3 cups)

1 can (about 14 ounces) chicken broth

2 cubes chicken bouillon

¼ teaspoon black pepper

¼ cup all-purpose flour

1½ cups milk

1½ cups (6 ounces) shredded Colby-Jack cheese

Chopped fresh parsley (optional)

1. Melt 2 tablespoons butter in large saucepan or Dutch oven over medium heat. Add onion slices; cook 10 minutes or until soft and translucent, stirring occasionally. Add broth, bouillon and pepper; cook until bouillon is dissolved and mixture is heated through.

2. Meanwhile, melt remaining 4 tablespoons butter in medium saucepan. Whisk in flour; cook and stir 1 minute. Gradually whisk in milk until well blended. Cook 10 minutes or until very thick, stirring occasionally.

3. Add milk mixture to soup; cook over medium-low heat 5 to 10 minutes or until thickened, stirring occasionally. Add cheese; cook 5 minutes or until melted and smooth. Ladle into bowls; garnish with parsley.

CHICKEN & BARLEY SOUP

MAKES 4 SERVINGS

1 cup thinly sliced celery

1 medium onion, coarsely chopped

1 carrot, thinly sliced

½ cup uncooked pearl barley

1 clove garlic, minced

1 cut-up whole chicken (about 3 pounds)

1 tablespoon olive oil

2½ cups chicken broth

1 can (about 14 ounces) diced tomatoes

¾ teaspoon salt

½ teaspoon dried basil

¼ teaspoon black pepper

SLOW COOKER DIRECTIONS

1. Combine celery, onion, carrot, barley and garlic in slow cooker.

2. Remove and discard skin from chicken. Separate drumsticks from thighs. Trim backbone from breasts. Save wings for another use. Heat oil in large skillet over medium-high heat; brown chicken on all sides. Place in slow cooker.

3. Add broth, tomatoes, salt, basil and pepper to slow cooker. Cover; cook on LOW 7 to 8 hours or on HIGH 4 hours or until chicken and barley are tender. Remove chicken to large cutting board; remove meat from bones. Cut chicken into 1-inch pieces; discard bones. Stir chicken into soup.

CORNED BEEF AND CABBAGE SOUP

MAKES ABOUT 8 SERVINGS

1 tablespoon vegetable oil

1 onion, chopped

2 stalks celery, chopped

2 carrots, chopped

2 cloves garlic, minced

4 to 5 cups coarsely chopped green cabbage (about half of small head)

12 ounces unpeeled Yukon gold potatoes, chopped

4 cups beef broth

4 cups water

½ cup quick-cooking barley

1 teaspoon salt

1 teaspoon dried thyme

½ teaspoon black pepper

¼ teaspoon ground mustard

12 ounces corned beef, cut into ½-inch pieces (leftovers or deli corned beef, about 2½ cups)

1. Heat oil in large saucepan or Dutch oven over medium-high heat. Add onion, celery and carrots; cook 5 minutes or until vegetables are softened, stirring occasionally. Add garlic; cook and stir 1 minute.

2. Stir in cabbage, potatoes, broth, water, barley, 1 teaspoon salt, thyme, ½ teaspoon pepper and mustard; bring to a boil. Reduce heat to medium-low. Cook 20 minutes, stirring occasionally.

3. Stir in corned beef; cook 10 to 15 minutes or until potatoes are tender. Season with additional salt and pepper, if desired.

CHICKEN NOODLE SOUP

MAKES 8 SERVINGS

2 tablespoons butter

1 cup chopped onion

1 cup sliced carrots

½ cup diced celery

2 tablespoons vegetable oil

1 pound chicken breast tenderloins

1 pound chicken thigh fillets

4 cups chicken broth, divided

2 cups water

1 tablespoon minced fresh parsley, plus additional for garnish

1½ teaspoons salt

½ teaspoon black pepper

3 cups uncooked egg noodles

1. Melt butter in large saucepan or Dutch oven over medium-low heat. Add onion, carrots and celery; cook 15 minutes or until vegetables are soft, stirring occasionally.

2. Meanwhile, heat oil in large skillet over medium-high heat. Add chicken in single layer; cook 12 minutes or until lightly browned and cooked through, turning once. Remove chicken to large cutting board. Add 1 cup broth to skillet; cook 1 minute, scraping up browned bits from bottom of skillet. Add broth to vegetables in saucepan. Stir in remaining 3 cups broth, water, 1 tablespoon parsley, salt and pepper.

3. Chop chicken into 1-inch pieces when cool enough to handle. Add to soup; bring to a boil over medium-high heat. Reduce heat to medium-low; cook 15 minutes. Add noodles; cook 15 minutes or until noodles are tender. Ladle into bowls; garnish with additional parsley.

SPLIT PEA SOUP

MAKES 6 SERVINGS

1 **package (16 ounces) dried green or yellow split peas**

7 **cups water**

1 **pound smoked ham hocks *or* 4 ounces smoked sausage links, sliced and quartered**

2 **carrots, chopped**

1 **onion, chopped**

¾ **teaspoon salt**

½ **teaspoon dried basil**

¼ **teaspoon dried oregano**

¼ **teaspoon black pepper**

1. Rinse split peas thoroughly in colander under cold running water; discard any debris or blemished peas.

2. Combine peas, water, ham hocks, carrots, onion, salt, basil, oregano and pepper in large saucepan or Dutch oven; bring to a boil over high heat. Reduce heat to medium-low. Simmer 1 hour 15 minutes or until peas are tender, stirring occasionally. Stir frequently near end of cooking to keep soup from scorching.

3. Remove ham hocks to large cutting board; let stand until cool enough to handle. Remove ham from hocks; chop meat and discard bones.

4. Place 3 cups soup in blender or food processor; blend until smooth. Return to saucepan; stir in ham. If soup is too thick, add water until desired consistency is reached. Cook just until heated through.

TIP: To purée soup, carefully pour the hot mixture into the blender. Cover with the lid, removing the center cap, then cover the hole with a towel. Start blending at low speed and gradually increase to high speed, blending to desired consistency.

¼ c
3 cl
¾ cup
2 eggs,
1 poun
1 po
1 c
2
½
⅓

SPAGHETTI & MEATBALLS

MAKES 4 SERVINGS

6 ounces uncooked multigrain or whole wheat spaghetti

¾ pound ground beef

¼ pound hot turkey Italian sausage, casing removed

1 egg

2 tablespoons plain dry bread crumbs

1 teaspoon dried oregano

2 cups tomato-basil pasta sauce

3 tablespoons chopped fresh basil

2 tablespoons grated Parmesan cheese

1. Preheat oven to 450°F. Spray baking sheet with nonstick cooking spray. Cook spaghetti according to package directions, omitting salt and fat. Drain and keep warm.

2. Combine beef, sausage, egg, bread crumbs and oregano in medium bowl; mix well. Shape mixture into 16 (1½-inch) meatballs. Place on prepared baking sheet; coat with cooking spray. Bake 12 minutes, turning once.

3. Pour pasta sauce into large skillet. Add meatballs; cook over medium heat 9 minutes or until sauce is heated through and meatballs are cooked through (160°F), stirring occasionally. Divide spaghetti among four plates. Top with meatballs and sauce; sprinkle with basil and cheese.

SWEET AND ZESTY SIRLOIN

MAKES 4 SERVINGS

¼ **cup steak sauce**

2 **tablespoons ketchup**

1 **tablespoon sugar**

1 **tablespoon balsamic vinegar**

2 **teaspoons grated orange peel**

¼ **teaspoon salt**

¼ **teaspoon red pepper flakes**

1½ **pounds boneless sirloin steak, about ¾ inch thick**

1. Combine steak sauce, ketchup, sugar, vinegar, orange peel, salt and red pepper flakes in small bowl; stir until well blended.

2. Place steak on large plate. Reserve 3 tablespoons sauce mixture. Pour remaining sauce mixture over steak, turning several times to coat evenly. Marinate 10 minutes. Preheat broiler.

3. Coat broiler rack with nonstick cooking spray. Place steak on rack. Broil 5 minutes; turn. Cook 5 minutes or until desired doneness.

4. Remove to large cutting board. Let stand 3 minutes. Slice diagonally and spoon reserved sauce over steak.

PORK CHOPS AND STUFFING SKILLET CASSEROLE

MAKES 4 SERVINGS

- **4 thin bone-in pork chops (1 pound)**
- **¼ teaspoon dried thyme**
- **¼ teaspoon paprika**
- **⅛ teaspoon salt**
- **¼ pound bulk pork sausage**
- **2 cups cornbread stuffing mix**
- **1¼ cups water**
- **1 cup frozen diced green bell peppers, thawed**
- **⅛ to ¼ teaspoon poultry seasoning (optional)**

1. Preheat oven to 350°F. Sprinkle one side of pork chops with thyme, paprika and salt. Spray large ovenproof skillet with nonstick cooking spray; heat over medium-high heat. Add pork, seasoned side down; cook 2 minutes. Remove to plate; keep warm.

2. Add sausage to skillet; cook 6 to 8 minutes or until no longer pink, stirring to break up meat. Remove from heat. Stir in stuffing mix, water, bell peppers and poultry seasoning, if desired, until just blended.

3. Arrange pork, seasoned side up, over stuffing mixture. Cover; bake 15 minutes or until pork is barely pink in center. Let stand 5 minutes before serving.

GRILLED REUBENS WITH COLESLAW

MAKES 4 SERVINGS

2 **cups sauerkraut**

¼ **cup (½ stick) butter, softened**

8 **slices marble rye or rye bread**

12 **ounces thinly sliced deli corned beef or pastrami**

¼ **to ½ cup Thousand Island dressing**

4 **slices Swiss cheese**

2 **cups deli coleslaw**

4 **kosher garlic pickle spears**

1. Preheat indoor grill or large grill pan. Drain sauerkraut well on paper towels.

2. Spread butter evenly over one side of each slice of bread. Turn 4 bread slices over; top evenly with corned beef, 1 to 2 tablespoons dressing, sauerkraut and cheese. Top with remaining 4 bread slices, butter side up.

3. Grill 4 minutes or just until cheese begins to melt. Serve with coleslaw and pickles.

NOTE: Stack sandwich ingredients in the order given to prevent sogginess.

POT ROAST

MAKES 6 TO 8 SERVINGS

1 tablespoon vegetable oil

1 boneless beef chuck shoulder roast (3 to 4 pounds)

6 medium potatoes, halved

6 medium carrots, cut into chunks

2 medium onions, quartered

2 stalks celery, sliced

1 can (about 14 ounces) diced tomatoes, undrained

Salt and black pepper

Dried oregano

Water

1½ to 2 tablespoons all-purpose flour

SLOW COOKER DIRECTIONS

1. Heat oil in large skillet over medium-low heat. Add roast; brown on all sides. Transfer to slow cooker.

2. Add potatoes, carrots, onions, celery and tomatoes with juice. Season with salt, pepper and oregano. Add enough water to cover bottom of slow cooker by about ½ inch. Cover; cook on LOW 8 to 10 hours. Remove roast to platter. Let stand 15 minutes.

3. Transfer juices to small saucepan. Whisk in flour until smooth. Cook and stir over medium heat until thickened. Slice roast and serve with gravy and vegetables.

HAM WITH SPICED COLA SAUCE

MAKES 10 TO 12 SERVINGS

1¼ cups packed dark brown sugar, divided

¾ cup cola, divided

3 tablespoons cider vinegar

1 tablespoon plus 1½ teaspoons grated orange peel

2 teaspoons ground cinnamon

1 teaspoon ground allspice

6 whole cloves

¼ teaspoon red pepper flakes

1 fully cooked bone-in ham (about 6 pounds)

2 tablespoons cornstarch

SLOW COOKER DIRECTIONS

1. Lightly coat slow cooker with nonstick cooking spray. Add 1 cup brown sugar, ½ cup cola, vinegar, orange peel, cinnamon, allspice, cloves and red pepper flakes; whisk until well blended. Place ham in slow cooker, cut side up. Cover; cook on LOW 5 hours or until ham is slightly separating from bone. Remove ham to large cutting board. Cover and let stand 20 minutes.

2. Meanwhile, strain drippings into large measuring cup. Let stand 5 minutes; skim and discard solids. Return drippings to slow cooker. Stir in remaining ¼ cup brown sugar.

3. *Turn slow cooker to HIGH.* Stir remaining ¼ cup cola into cornstarch in small bowl until smooth. Whisk into slow cooker. Cover; cook on HIGH 20 minutes or until thickened. Serve sauce with ham.

HERBED PORK WITH POTATOES AND GREEN BEANS

MAKES 4 SERVINGS

2 tablespoons chopped fresh thyme

2 tablespoons chopped fresh rosemary

2 cloves garlic, minced

2 teaspoons salt

¾ teaspoon black pepper

¼ cup olive oil

1½ pounds (about 18) fingerling potatoes, cut in half lengthwise (2- to 3-inch)

1 pound green beans

2 pork tenderloins (about 12 ounces each)

1. Preheat oven to 450°F. Combine thyme, rosemary, garlic, salt and pepper in small bowl. Stir in oil until well blended.

2. Place potatoes in medium bowl. Drizzle with one third of oil mixture, toss to coat. Arrange potatoes, cut sides down, in rows covering two thirds of baking sheet. (Potatoes should be in single layer; do not overlap.) Leave remaining one third of baking sheet empty.

3. Roast potatoes 10 minutes while preparing beans and pork. Trim green beans; place in same bowl used for potatoes. Drizzle with one third of oil mixture; toss to coat. When potatoes have roasted for 10 minutes, remove baking sheet from oven. Arrange green beans on empty one third of baking sheet. Brush all sides of pork with remaining oil mixture; place on top of green beans.

4. Roast 20 to 25 minutes or until pork is 145°F. Remove pork to large cutting board; tent with foil and let stand 10 minutes. Stir vegetables; return to oven. Roast 10 minutes or until golden brown. Slice pork; serve with vegetables.

POULTRY

SIMPLE ROASTED CHICKEN

MAKES 4 SERVINGS

1 **whole chicken (about 4 pounds)**

3 **tablespoons butter, softened**

1½ **teaspoons salt**

1 **teaspoon onion powder**

1 **teaspoon dried thyme**

½ **teaspoon garlic powder**

½ **teaspoon paprika**

½ **teaspoon black pepper**

Fresh parsley sprigs and lemon wedges (optional)

1. Preheat oven to 425°F. Pat chicken dry; place in small baking dish or on baking sheet.

2. Combine butter, salt, onion powder, thyme, garlic powder, paprika and pepper in small microwavable bowl; mash with fork until well blended. Loosen skin on breasts and thighs; spread about one third of butter mixture under skin.

3. Microwave remaining butter mixture until melted. Brush melted butter mixture all over outside of chicken and inside cavity. Tie drumsticks together with kitchen string and tuck wing tips under.

4. Roast 20 minutes. *Reduce oven temperature to 375°F.* Roast 45 to 55 minutes or until chicken is cooked through (165°F), basting once with pan juices during last 10 minutes of cooking time. Remove chicken to large cutting board; tent with foil. Let stand at least 15 minutes before carving. Garnish with parsley and lemon, if desired.

SOUTHWEST TURKEY BAKE

MAKES 8 SERVINGS

1 **pound ground turkey**

1 **can (about 15 ounces) black beans, rinsed and drained**

1 **cup salsa**

½ **teaspoon ground cumin**

⅛ **teaspoon ground red pepper**

1 **package (8½ ounces) corn muffin mix**

¾ **cup chicken broth**

1 **egg**

¾ **cup (3 ounces) shredded Mexican cheese blend**

Lime wedges (optional)

1. Preheat oven to 400°F. Brown turkey in large nonstick skillet over medium-high heat 6 to 8 minutes or until no longer pink, stirring to break up meat. Stir in beans, salsa, cumin and red pepper; simmer 2 minutes.

2. Spoon turkey mixture into 13×9-inch baking dish.

3. Combine corn muffin mix, broth and egg in medium bowl; mix well. Spread over turkey mixture. Sprinkle evenly with cheese.

4. Bake 15 minutes or until edges are lightly browned. Serve with lime wedges, if desired.

TIP: Ground turkey can tend to dry out, so it is best used in recipes when mixed with a liquid ingredient such as salsa.

CRISPY BUTTERMILK FRIED CHICKEN

MAKES 4 SERVINGS

2 cups buttermilk

1 tablespoon hot pepper sauce

3 pounds bone-in chicken pieces

2 cups all-purpose flour

2 teaspoons salt

2 teaspoons poultry seasoning

1 teaspoon garlic salt

1 teaspoon paprika

1 teaspoon ground red pepper

1 teaspoon black pepper

1 cup vegetable oil

1. Combine buttermilk and hot pepper sauce in large resealable food storage bag. Add chicken; seal bag. Turn to coat. Refrigerate 2 hours or up to 24 hours.

2. Combine flour, salt, poultry seasoning, garlic salt, paprika, red pepper and black pepper in another large resealable food storage bag or shallow baking dish; mix well. Working in batches, remove chicken from buttermilk; shake off excess. Add to flour mixture; shake to coat.

3. Heat oil over medium heat in heavy deep skillet until deep-fry thermometer registers 350°F. Working in batches, fry chicken 30 minutes or until cooked through (165°F), turning occasionally to brown all sides. Drain on paper towels.

NOTE: Carefully monitor the temperature of the oil during cooking. It should not drop below 325°F or go higher than 350°F. The chicken can also be cooked in a deep fryer following the manufacturer's directions. Never leave hot oil unattended.

OLD-FASHIONED CHICKEN WITH DUMPLINGS

MAKES 6 SERVINGS

3 tablespoons butter

3 to 3½ pounds chicken pieces

3 cans (about 14 ounces each) chicken broth

3½ cups water

1 teaspoon salt

¼ teaspoon white pepper

2 large carrots, cut into 1-inch slices

2 stalks celery, cut into 1-inch slices

8 to 10 pearl onions, peeled

¼ pound small mushrooms, cut into halves

Parsley Dumplings (recipe follows)

½ cup frozen peas, thawed and drained

1. Melt butter in 6- to 8-quart Dutch oven over medium-high heat. Add chicken; cook until golden brown on all sides.

2. Add broth, water, salt and pepper; bring to a boil over high heat. Reduce heat to low; cover and simmer 15 minutes. Add carrots, celery, onions and mushrooms; cover and simmer 40 minutes or until chicken and vegetables are tender.

3. Prepare Parsley Dumplings. When chicken is tender, skim fat from broth. Stir in peas. Drop dumpling mixture into broth, making 12 dumplings. Cover; simmer 15 to 20 minutes or until dumplings are firm to the touch and toothpick inserted into centers comes out clean.

PARSLEY DUMPLINGS: Sift 2 cups all-purpose flour, 4 teaspoons baking powder and 1 teaspoon salt into medium bowl. Cut in 5 tablespoons cold butter with pastry blender or two knives until mixture resembles coarse meal. Make well in center; pour in 1 cup milk. Add 2 tablespoons chopped fresh parsley; stir with fork until mixture forms ball.

JERK TURKEY STEW

MAKES 4 SERVINGS

1 tablespoon vegetable oil

1 small red onion, chopped

1 clove garlic, minced

½ teaspoon ground ginger

¼ teaspoon salt

¼ teaspoon black pepper

⅛ to ¼ teaspoon ground red pepper*

⅛ teaspoon ground allspice

1 can (about 28 ounces) diced tomatoes

3 cups diced cooked turkey

2 cups diced cooked sweet potato (½-inch pieces)

½ cup turkey broth or gravy

1 tablespoon lime juice

1 tablespoon minced fresh chives

*Use ⅛ teaspoon for a mildly spicy dish; use ¼ teaspoon for a very spicy dish.

1. Heat oil in Dutch oven over medium heat. Add onion and garlic; cook and stir 5 minutes. Add ginger, salt, black pepper, red pepper and allspice; cook 20 seconds. Stir in tomatoes, turkey, sweet potatoes and broth. Reduce heat to low; simmer 15 minutes.

2. Stir in lime juice; cover and let stand 10 minutes. Sprinkle with chives just before serving.

TIP: Instead of sweet potatoes, add a cooked diced white potato or simply serve this stew over cooked rice.

COUNTRY CHICKEN POT PIE

MAKES 6 SERVINGS

2 tablespoons butter

1 pound boneless skinless chicken breasts, cut into 1-inch pieces

¾ teaspoon salt

8 ounces fresh green beans, cut into 1-inch pieces (about 2 cups)

½ cup chopped red bell pepper

½ cup thinly sliced celery

3 tablespoons rice flour

½ cup chicken broth

½ cup half-and-half

1 teaspoon dried thyme

½ teaspoon dried sage

1 cup frozen pearl onions

½ cup frozen corn

1 (10-inch) prepared pie crust

1. Preheat oven to 425°F. Spray 10-inch deep-dish pie plate with nonstick cooking spray.

2. Melt butter in large skillet over medium-high heat. Add chicken; cook and stir 3 minutes or until no longer pink in center. Sprinkle with salt. Add green beans, bell pepper and celery; cook and stir 3 minutes or until vegetables are crisp-tender.

3. Sprinkle rice flour evenly over chicken and vegetables; cook and stir 1 minute. Stir in broth, half-and-half, thyme and sage; bring to a boil over high heat. Reduce heat to low. Simmer 3 minutes or until sauce is thickened. Stir in onions and corn. Return to a simmer; cook and stir 1 minute.

4. Remove mixture to prepared pie plate. Place prepared pie crust over chicken mixture; turn edge under and crimp to seal. Cut slits out of pie crust to allow steam to escape.

5. Bake 25 minutes or until crust is light golden brown and mixture is hot and bubbly. Let stand 5 minutes before serving.

MOM'S BEST CHICKEN TETRAZZINI

MAKES 6 SERVINGS

8 ounces uncooked thin noodles or vermicelli pasta

2 tablespoons butter

8 ounces mushrooms, sliced

¼ cup chopped green onions

1 can (about 14 ounces) chicken broth

1 cup half-and-half, divided

2 tablespoons dry sherry

¼ cup all-purpose flour

½ teaspoon salt

¼ teaspoon ground nutmeg

⅛ teaspoon white pepper

1 jar (2 ounces) chopped pimientos, drained

½ cup grated Parmesan cheese, divided

½ cup sour cream

2 cups cubed cooked chicken

1. Preheat oven to 350°F. Spray 1½-quart casserole with nonstick cooking spray. Cook noodles according to package directions; drain.

2. Meanwhile, melt butter in large nonstick skillet over medium-high heat. Add mushrooms and green onions; cook and stir until green onions are tender. Stir in broth, ½ cup half-and-half and sherry.

3. Pour remaining ½ cup half-and-half into small jar with tight-fitting lid. Add flour, salt, nutmeg and pepper; shake until well blended. Slowly stir flour mixture into skillet. Bring to a boil; cook 1 minute. Reduce heat to low; stir in pimientos, ¼ cup cheese and sour cream. Add chicken and noodles; mix well. Remove to prepared casserole; sprinkle with remaining ¼ cup cheese.

4. Bake 30 to 35 minutes or until heated through.

BBQ CHICKEN SKILLET PIZZA

MAKES 4 TO 6 SERVINGS

1 pound frozen bread dough, thawed

1 tablespoon olive oil

2 cups shredded cooked chicken*

¾ cup barbecue sauce, divided

¼ cup (1 ounce) shredded mozzarella cheese

¼ cup thinly sliced red onion

½ cup (2 ounces) shredded smoked Gouda

Chopped fresh cilantro (optional)

*Use a rotisserie chicken for best flavor and convenience.

1. Preheat oven to 425°F. Roll out dough into 15-inch circle on lightly floured surface. Brush oil over bottom and side of large (12-inch) cast iron skillet; place in oven 5 minutes to preheat.

2. Combine chicken and ½ cup barbecue sauce in medium bowl; toss to coat. Remove hot skillet from oven; press dough into bottom and about 1 inch up side of skillet.

3. Spread remaining ¼ cup barbecue sauce over dough. Sprinkle with mozzarella cheese; top with chicken mixture. Sprinkle with half of onion and Gouda cheese; top with remaining onion.

4. Bake 25 minutes or until crust is golden brown. Garnish with cilantro.

SOFT TURKEY TACOS

MAKES 4 SERVINGS

8 **(6-inch) corn or flour tortillas**

1½ **teaspoons vegetable oil**

1 **pound ground turkey**

1 **small onion, chopped**

1 **teaspoon dried oregano**

Salt and black pepper

Optional toppings: chopped tomatoes, shredded lettuce and/or salsa

1. Wrap tortillas in foil. Place in cold oven; set temperature to 350°F.

2. Heat oil in large skillet over medium heat. Add turkey and onion; cook 6 to 8 minutes until turkey is no longer pink, stirring occasionally. Stir in oregano. Season with salt and pepper to taste. Keep warm.

3. For each taco, fill warm tortilla with turkey mixture; top as desired.

NOTE: To warm tortillas in microwave oven, wrap loosely in damp paper towel. Microwave on HIGH 2 minutes or until warm.

CHICKEN AND HERB STEW

MAKES 4 SERVINGS

½ cup all-purpose flour

½ teaspoon salt

¼ teaspoon black pepper

¼ teaspoon paprika

4 chicken drumsticks

4 chicken thighs

2 tablespoons olive oil

12 ounces unpeeled new red potatoes, quartered

2 carrots, quartered lengthwise, then cut crosswise into 3-inch pieces

1 green bell pepper, cut into thin strips

¾ cup chopped onion

2 cloves garlic, minced

1¾ cups water

¼ cup dry white wine

2 cubes chicken bouillon

1 tablespoon chopped fresh oregano

1 teaspoon chopped fresh rosemary leaves

2 tablespoons chopped fresh Italian parsley (optional)

1. Combine flour, salt, black pepper and paprika in shallow dish; stir until well blended. Coat chicken with flour mixture; shake off excess.

2. Heat oil in large skillet over medium-high heat. Add chicken; cook 10 minutes or until browned on both sides, turning once. Remove to plate.

3. Add potatoes, carrots, bell pepper, onion and garlic to skillet; cook 6 minutes or until vegetables are lightly browned, stirring occasionally. Add water, wine and bouillon; cook 1 minute, scraping up browned bits from bottom of skillet. Stir in oregano and rosemary.

4. Place chicken on top of vegetable mixture, turning several times to coat. Cover; simmer 45 to 50 minutes or until chicken is cooked through (165°F), turning occasionally. Garnish with parsley.

SEAFOOD

CORNMEAL-CRUSTED CATFISH

MAKES 4 SERVINGS

½ **cup cornmeal**

¼ **cup crushed pecans**

2 **teaspoons dried minced onion**

1½ **teaspoons garlic powder**

1 **teaspoon salt**

1 **teaspoon paprika**

½ **teaspoon black pepper**

3 **tablespoons mayonnaise**

2 **tablespoons apricot preserves or fruit spread**

1 **pound catfish fillets**

1. Heat medium nonstick skillet over medium heat. Add cornmeal, pecans, onion, garlic powder, salt, paprika and pepper; cook and stir 3 minutes or until cornmeal begins to brown. Remove to shallow dish.

2. Combine mayonnaise and preserves in small bowl or cup. Coat catfish with mayonnaise mixture. Dredge in toasted cornmeal mixture; turn to coat.

3. Spray same skillet with nonstick cooking spray; heat over medium heat. Add catfish; cook 3 to 4 minutes on each side or until fish begins to flake when tested with fork.

SALMON & NOODLE CASSEROLE

MAKES 4 SERVINGS

6 ounces uncooked wide egg noodles

1 teaspoon vegetable oil

1 onion, finely chopped

¾ cup thinly sliced carrot

¾ cup thinly sliced celery

1 can (about 15 ounces) salmon, drained, skin and bones discarded

1 can (10¾ ounces) condensed cream of celery soup, undiluted

1 cup (4 ounces) shredded Cheddar cheese

¾ cup frozen peas

½ cup sour cream

¼ cup milk

2 teaspoons dried dill weed

Black pepper

Chopped fresh dill (optional)

1. Preheat oven to 350°F.

2. Cook noodles according to package directions; drain and return to saucepan.

3. Heat oil in large skillet over medium heat. Add onion, carrot and celery; cook and stir 5 minutes or until carrot is crisp-tender. Add to noodles with salmon, soup, cheese, peas, sour cream, milk, dill weed and pepper; stir gently to coat. Pour into 2-quart baking dish.

4. Cover; bake 25 minutes or until hot and bubbly. Garnish with fresh dill.

SEAFOOD GUMBO

MAKES 4 TO 6 SERVINGS

½ teaspoon garlic powder

½ teaspoon onion powder

½ teaspoon black pepper

⅛ teaspoon dried thyme

2 tablespoons olive oil

2 tablespoons all-purpose flour

2½ cups diced onions

1½ cups diced celery

¾ cup diced red bell pepper

1 clove garlic, finely minced

1 teaspoon hot pepper sauce

1 teaspoon red pepper flakes

3 cups chicken broth

1 cup canned crushed tomatoes

6 okra, sliced

6 slices hot coppa,* chopped and fried

1 small can smoked oysters, rinsed and drained

1 cup lump crabmeat

1 cup small raw shrimp

2 fresh plum tomatoes, seeded and chopped

Salt and black pepper

2 cups cooked white rice

*Coppa (capicola or capicollo) is a cured meat much like salami.

1. Combine garlic powder, onion powder, ½ teaspoon black pepper and thyme in small bowl; mix well.

2. Heat oil in large saucepan or Dutch oven over medium-low heat. Stir in flour until blended. Cook 5 minutes or until flour mixture (roux) is deep golden brown.

3. Add onions, celery and bell pepper; cook over medium-high heat 5 minutes or until vegetables are tender. Add garlic; cook and stir 1 minute. Stir in spice mixture, hot pepper sauce and red pepper flakes. Add broth and crushed tomatoes; bring to a boil over high heat. Stir in okra. Reduce heat to low; cook, uncovered, 40 minutes.

4. Stir in coppa, oysters, crabmeat, shrimp and plum tomatoes. Cover; cook over low heat 30 minutes. Season with salt and additional black pepper. Serve over rice.

BLACKENED SHRIMP WITH TOMATOES

MAKES 4 SERVINGS

1½ teaspoons paprika

1 teaspoon Italian seasoning

½ teaspoon garlic powder

¼ teaspoon black pepper

½ pound (about 24) small raw shrimp, peeled (with tails on)

1 tablespoon canola oil

1½ cups halved grape tomatoes

½ cup sliced onion, separated into rings

Lime wedges (optional)

1. Combine paprika, Italian seasoning, garlic powder and pepper in small bowl; add to large resealable food storage bag. Add shrimp, seal bag and shake to coat.

2. Heat oil in large skillet over medium-high heat. Add shrimp; cook 4 minutes or until shrimp are pink and opaque, turning occasionally.

3. Add tomatoes and onion to skillet; cook 1 minute or until tomatoes are heated through and onion is softened. Serve with lime wedges, if desired.

SOUTHWEST ROASTED SALMON & CORN

MAKES 2 SERVINGS

2 **medium ears fresh corn, unhusked**

1 **salmon fillet (6 ounces), cut in half**

1 **tablespoon plus 1 teaspoon lime juice, divided**

1 **clove garlic, minced**

½ **teaspoon chili powder**

¼ **teaspoon ground cumin**

¼ **teaspoon dried oregano**

⅛ **teaspoon salt, divided**

⅛ **teaspoon black pepper**

2 **teaspoons butter, melted**

2 **teaspoons minced fresh cilantro**

1. Pull back husks from each ear of corn, leaving attached. Discard silk. Bring husks back up over each ear. Soak corn in cold water 20 minutes.

2. Preheat oven to 400°F. Spray shallow 1-quart baking dish with nonstick cooking spray. Place salmon, skin side down, in prepared dish. Pour 1 tablespoon lime juice over fish. Marinate at room temperature 15 minutes.

3. Combine garlic, chili powder, cumin, oregano, half of salt and pepper in small bowl. Pat salmon lightly with paper towel; rub garlic mixture over salmon.

4. Remove corn from water. Place corn directly on oven rack. Roast 10 minutes; turn. Place salmon in baking dish next to corn. Roast 15 minutes or until salmon is opaque and flakes when tested with fork and corn is tender.

5. Combine butter, cilantro, remaining 1 teaspoon lime juice and remaining salt in small bowl. Remove husks from corn. Brush over corn. Serve corn with salmon.

TIP: Corn can also be cooked in boiling water. Omit steps 1 and 4. Husk the corn and place in a large pot of boiling water. Cover; remove from heat and let stand for 10 minutes. Drain and brush with cilantro butter as directed.

BUTTERY CRACKER AND OYSTER CASSEROLE

MAKES 12 SERVINGS

3 sleeves saltine crackers (about 110 crackers total)

1 container (16 ounces) oysters (about 18 oysters total), drained

1 cup (2 sticks) butter, cut into ½-inch cubes, divided

3 cups whole milk, divided

1. Preheat oven to 350°F.

2. Coat 13×9-inch glass baking dish with nonstick cooking spray. Coarsely crush crackers in packages with hands. (Most crumbs should be in ½-inch pieces.) Break seal of one sleeve; sprinkle crumbs into bottom of prepared baking dish. Arrange half of oysters on top of crumbs. Drop about one fourth of butter cubes over oysters; drizzle 1½ cups milk over all. Repeat layers. Sprinkle with remaining sleeve of crackers and top with remaining butter.

3. Bake, uncovered, 30 minutes or until light golden brown. Let stand 10 minutes before serving. Serve within 30 minutes for peak flavor and texture.

SHRIMP CREOLE

MAKES 4 TO 6 SERVINGS

2 tablespoons olive oil

1½ cups chopped green bell peppers

1 medium onion, chopped

⅔ cup chopped celery

2 cloves garlic, minced

1 cup uncooked rice

1 can (about 14 ounces) diced tomatoes, drained and liquid reserved

2 teaspoons hot pepper sauce, or to taste

1 teaspoon dried oregano

¾ teaspoon salt

½ teaspoon dried thyme

Black pepper

1 pound medium raw shrimp, peeled and deveined (with tails on)

1 tablespoon chopped fresh parsley (optional)

1. Preheat oven to 325°F. Heat oil in large skillet over medium-high heat. Add bell peppers, onion, celery and garlic; cook and stir 5 minutes or until vegetables are tender.

2. Add rice; cook and stir over medium heat 5 minutes. Add tomatoes, hot pepper sauce, oregano, salt, thyme and black pepper to skillet; stir until well blended.

3. Pour reserved tomato liquid into measuring cup; add enough water to measure 1¾ cups. Add to skillet; cook and stir 2 minutes. Stir in shrimp. Remove to 2½-quart casserole.

4. Cover; bake 55 minutes or until rice is tender and liquid is absorbed. Garnish with parsley.

TUNA TOMATO CASSEROLE

MAKES 6 SERVINGS

2 cans (6 ounces each) tuna, drained and flaked

1 cup mayonnaise

1 onion, finely chopped

¼ teaspoon salt

¼ teaspoon black pepper

1 package (12 ounces) wide egg noodles, uncooked

8 to 10 plum tomatoes, sliced ¼ inch thick

1 cup (4 ounces) shredded Cheddar or mozzarella cheese

1. Preheat oven to 375°F.

2. Combine tuna, mayonnaise, onion, salt and pepper in medium bowl; mix well.

3. Cook noodles according to package directions; drain and return to saucepan. Gently stir in tuna mixture until well blended. Layer half of noodle mixture, half of tomatoes and half of cheese in 13×9-inch baking dish; press down slightly. Repeat layers.

4. Bake 20 minutes or until cheese is melted and casserole is heated through.

STEWED OKRA & SHRIMP

MAKES 4 SERVINGS

½ **pound okra**

1 **teaspoon canola or vegetable oil**

½ **cup finely chopped onion**

1 **can (about 14 ounces) stewed tomatoes, undrained, chopped**

1 **teaspoon dried thyme**

¼ **teaspoon salt**

¾ **cup fresh corn kernels or thawed frozen corn**

½ **teaspoon hot pepper sauce**

2 **ounces cooked baby shrimp**

1. Remove and discard tip and stem ends from okra. Cut okra into ½-inch slices.

2. Heat oil in large nonstick skillet over medium heat. Add onion; cook and stir 3 minutes. Add okra; cook and stir 3 minutes. Add tomatoes with juice, thyme and salt; bring to a boil over high heat. Reduce heat to low; cover and simmer 10 minutes.

3. Add corn and hot pepper sauce; cover and simmer 10 minutes. Add shrimp; cook and stir until heated through.

MAPLE SALMON AND SWEETS

MAKES 4 SERVINGS

½ **cup pure maple syrup**

2 **tablespoons butter, melted**

1½ **pounds skin-on salmon
fillets**

2 **medium sweet potatoes,
peeled and cut into
¼-inch slices**

1 **teaspoon salt**

¼ **teaspoon black pepper**

1. Combine maple syrup and butter in small bowl; mix well. Place salmon in large resealable food storage bag. Place sweet potatoes in another large resealable food storage bag. Pour half of syrup mixture into each bag; seal bags and turn to coat. Refrigerate at least 2 hours or overnight, turning occasionally.

2. Prepare grill for direct cooking. Oil grid. Drain salmon and sweet potatoes; discard marinade. Season with salt and pepper.

3. Grill salmon, skin-side down, on covered grill over medium heat 15 to 20 minutes or until fish begins to flake when tested with fork. (Do not turn.) Grill sweet potatoes, covered, in single layer on grill topper 15 minutes or until tender and slightly browned, turning once or twice.

SIDES

BACON-JALAPEÑO CORNBREAD

MAKES 9 TO 12 SERVINGS

- **4 slices bacon**
- **¼ cup minced green onions**
- **2 jalapeño peppers, seeded and minced**
- **1 cup all-purpose flour**
- **1 cup yellow cornmeal**
- **2½ teaspoons baking powder**
- **¾ teaspoon salt**
- **½ teaspoon baking soda**
- **1 egg**
- **¾ cup plain yogurt**
- **¾ cup milk**
- **¼ cup (½ stick) butter, melted**
- **½ cup (2 ounces) shredded Cheddar cheese**

1. Preheat oven to 400°F.

2. Cook bacon in large skillet over medium heat until crisp. Drain on paper towel-lined plate. Pour 2 tablespoons drippings into 9-inch square baking pan or cast iron skillet.

3. Crumble bacon into small bowl; add green onions and jalapeños. Combine flour, cornmeal, baking powder, salt and baking soda in large bowl.

4. Beat egg lightly in medium bowl; add yogurt and whisk until smooth. Whisk in milk and butter. Add to flour mixture; stir just until moistened. Stir in bacon mixture. Pour into prepared pan; sprinkle with cheese.

5. Bake 20 to 25 minutes or until toothpick inserted into center comes out clean. Cut into squares or wedges.

GARLIC CHEDDAR GRITS

MAKES 8 SERVINGS

2 tablespoons butter

2 cloves garlic, minced

4 cups (32 ounces) vegetable or chicken broth*

1 cup grits (not instant)

2 cups (8 ounces) shredded sharp Cheddar cheese, plus additional for topping

2 eggs

¼ to ½ teaspoon salt

Hot pepper sauce or ground red pepper

*This amount of broth will produce creamy grits. For a firmer texture, reduce broth to 3½ cups.

1. Melt butter in large heavy saucepan over medium-high heat. Add garlic; cook and stir 30 seconds. Add broth; bring to a boil over high heat. Stir in grits; reduce heat to low. Cover and simmer 15 minutes or until creamy, stirring twice.

2. Meanwhile, preheat oven to 375°F. Lightly grease 1½-quart casserole or 9-inch deep-dish pie plate.

3. Remove grits from heat; stir in 2 cups cheese until melted. Beat eggs in small bowl until thick and pale yellow. Stir 1 spoonful of grits mixture into eggs until well blended. Fold egg mixture into remaining grits mixture until evenly blended. Season to taste with salt and hot pepper sauce. Spoon into prepared casserole.

4. Bake, uncovered, 40 to 45 minutes or until golden brown and center is set. Top with additional cheese, if desired.

CORNBREAD, BACON AND SAGE DRESSING

MAKES 8 SERVINGS

1 package (6½ ounces) cornbread mix

⅓ cup milk

2 egg whites

2 tablespoons plus 1 teaspoon canola oil, divided

1 cup diced onion (1 medium onion)

¾ cup diced celery (2 stalks)

2 tablespoons bacon bits, plus additional for garnish

1 teaspoon ground sage

½ teaspoon sweet paprika

¼ teaspoon salt

¼ teaspoon black pepper

1¼ cups chicken broth

1. Preheat oven to 400°F. Lightly spray 8-inch square baking pan with nonstick cooking spray.

2. Combine cornbread mix, milk, egg whites and 2 tablespoons oil in medium bowl, stirring just until moistened. (Mixture will be lumpy.) Pour batter into prepared pan.

3. Bake 15 to 16 minutes or until firm and brown on edges. Cool cornbread in pan on wire rack. Crumble cooled cornbread onto baking sheet. Let stand 1 to 2 hours or until slightly dry.

4. Preheat oven to 350°F. Heat remaining 1 teaspoon oil in large deep skillet over medium heat. Add onion and celery; cook and stir 3 to 4 minutes or until onion is translucent and celery is crisp-tender. Do not brown. Stir in 2 tablespoons bacon bits, sage, paprika, salt and pepper. Remove skillet from heat. Gently fold in dried cornbread, keeping mixture light and fluffy. Pour broth over mixture, fluffing lightly with fork. Spoon dressing into prepared pan; sprinkle with additional bacon bits, if desired.

5. Bake 20 minutes or until top is slightly crusty.

CLASSIC MACARONI AND CHEESE

MAKES 8 SERVINGS (ABOUT 8 CUPS)

2 cups uncooked elbow macaroni

¼ cup (½ stick) butter

¼ cup all-purpose flour

2½ cups whole milk

1 teaspoon salt

⅛ teaspoon black pepper

4 cups (16 ounces) shredded Colby-Jack cheese

1. Cook pasta according to package directions until al dente; drain.

2. Melt butter in large saucepan over medium heat. Add flour; whisk until well blended and bubbly. Gradually add milk, salt and pepper, whisking until blended. Cook and stir until milk begins to bubble. Add cheese, 1 cup at a time; cook and stir until cheese is melted and sauce is smooth.

3. Add cooked pasta to saucepan; stir gently until blended. Cook until heated through.

BARLEY & MUSHROOM PILAF

MAKES 4 SERVINGS

1 cup chicken broth

½ cup quick cooking barley

1 cup chopped onion

4 ounces sliced mushrooms

1 medium clove garlic, minced

½ teaspoon dried oregano

2 teaspoons olive oil

¼ teaspoon salt

⅛ teaspoon black pepper

Chopped fresh parsley

1. Bring broth to a boil in medium saucepan over high heat. Stir in barley. Reduce heat to low. Simmer, covered, 10 minutes. Set aside.

2. Meanwhile, spray 12-inch skillet with nonstick cooking spray. Heat over medium-high heat. Cook and stir onion 4 minutes or until tender. Add mushrooms, garlic and oregano; cook and stir 4 minutes or until mushrooms begin to brown.

3. Remove from heat. Stir into barley with oil, salt and pepper. Sprinkle with parsley; serve immediately.

CLASSIC MACARONI AND CHEESE

SUPER SIMPLE CHEESY BUBBLE LOAF

MAKES 12 SERVINGS

- 2 **packages (12 ounces each) refrigerated buttermilk biscuits (10 biscuits per package)**
- 2 **tablespoons butter, melted**
- 1½ **cups (6 ounces) shredded Italian cheese blend**

1. Preheat oven to 350°F. Spray 9×5-inch loaf pan with nonstick cooking spray.

2. Separate biscuits; cut each biscuit into four pieces with scissors. Layer half of biscuit pieces in prepared pan. Drizzle with 1 tablespoon butter; sprinkle with 1 cup cheese. Top with remaining biscuit pieces, 1 tablespoon butter and ½ cup cheese.

3. Bake about 25 minutes or until golden brown. Serve warm.

TIP: It's easy to change up the flavors in this simple bread. Try Mexican cheese blend instead of Italian, and add taco seasoning and/or hot pepper sauce to the melted butter before drizzling it over the dough. Or, sprinkle ¼ cup chopped ham, salami or crumbled crisp-cooked bacon between the layers of dough.

GARDEN VEGETABLE PASTA SALAD WITH BACON

MAKES 6 TO 8 SERVINGS

12 ounces uncooked rotini pasta

2 cups broccoli florets

1 can (about 14 ounces) diced tomatoes

2 medium carrots, diagonally sliced

2 stalks celery, sliced

10 medium mushrooms, thinly sliced

½ medium red onion, thinly sliced

½ pound bacon, crisp-cooked and crumbled

1 bottle (8 ounces) Italian or ranch salad dressing

½ cup (2 ounces) shredded Cheddar cheese

1 tablespoon dried parsley flakes

2 teaspoons dried basil

¼ teaspoon black pepper

1. Cook pasta according to package directions. Drain and rinse well under cold running water until cool.

2. Combine broccoli, tomatoes, carrots, celery, mushrooms and onion in large bowl. Add pasta and bacon; toss lightly.

3. Add salad dressing, cheese, parsley flakes, basil and pepper; stir to combine.

DINNER ROLLS

MAKES 24 ROLLS

1¼ cups milk

½ cup shortening

3¾ to 4¼ cups all-purpose flour, divided

¼ cup sugar

2 packages (¼ ounce each) active dry yeast

1 teaspoon salt

2 eggs

1. Combine milk and shortening in small saucepan. Heat over low heat until temperature reaches 120° to 130°F. (Shortening does not need to melt completely.)

2. Combine 1½ cups flour, sugar, yeast and salt in large bowl. Gradually beat milk mixture into flour mixture with electric mixer at low speed until well combined. Beat in eggs and 1 cup flour; beat at medium speed 2 minutes. Using wooden spoon, stir in enough additional flour to make soft dough, about 1¼ cups.

3. Turn out dough onto lightly floured surface. Knead in enough remaining flour until dough is smooth and elastic. (This takes about 10 minutes.)

4. Place dough in large, lightly greased bowl; turn once to coat evenly. Cover with towel; let rise in warm place 1 hour or until doubled in size.

5. Punch down dough. Knead on lightly floured surface 1 minute. Cover with towel; let rest 10 minutes. Grease two 8-inch square baking pans. Cut dough in half. Cut one half into 12 pieces, keeping remaining half covered with towel. Shape pieces into balls; place in rows in one prepared pan. Repeat with remaining dough. Cover pans with towels; let rise in warm place (85°F) 30 minutes or until doubled in size.

6. Preheat oven to 375°F. Bake 15 to 20 minutes or until golden brown. Remove to wire racks to cool slightly. Serve warm.

PESTO RICE AND BEANS

MAKES 8 SERVINGS

1 can (about 15 ounces) Great Northern beans, rinsed and drained

1 can (about 14 ounces) vegetable broth

¾ cup uncooked long grain white rice

1½ cups frozen cut green beans, thawed and drained

½ cup prepared pesto

Grated Parmesan cheese (optional)

SLOW COOKER DIRECTIONS

1. Combine Great Northern beans, broth and rice in slow cooker. Cover; cook on LOW 2 hours.

2. Stir in green beans; cover and cook on LOW 1 hour or until rice and beans are tender.

3. Turn off heat and remove insert to heatproof surface. Stir in pesto and cheese, if desired. Let stand, covered, 5 minutes or until cheese is melted. Serve immediately.

HUSH PUPPIES

MAKES ABOUT 24 HUSH PUPPIES

1½ **cups yellow cornmeal**

½ **cup all-purpose flour**

2 **teaspoons baking powder**

¾ **teaspoon salt**

1 **cup milk**

1 **small onion, minced**

1 **egg, lightly beaten**

Vegetable oil

Ketchup (optional)

1. Combine cornmeal, flour, baking powder and salt in medium bowl; mix well. Add milk, onion and egg; stir until well blended. Let batter stand 5 to 10 minutes.

2. Heat 1 inch of oil in large heavy skillet over medium heat to 375°F; adjust heat to maintain temperature. Drop batter by tablespoonfuls into hot oil. Cook, in batches, 2 minutes or until golden brown. Drain on paper towel-lined plate. Serve warm with ketchup, if desired.

SPICY BLACK-EYED PEAS WITH HAM HOCKS

MAKES 6 SERVINGS

6 **cups water**

2 **ham hocks (about 1 pound)**

2 **pounds frozen black-eyed peas**

½ **cup chopped onion**

½ **medium jalapeño pepper, stemmed and sliced in rounds**

2 **teaspoons salt**

Sliced green onions

1. Bring water to a boil over high heat in Dutch oven. Add ham hocks, black-eyed peas, onion, jalapeño and salt; return to a boil. Reduce heat to low. Simmer, uncovered, 30 minutes or until peas are very tender and mixture begins to thicken slightly.

2. Remove from heat and remove ham hocks. Let stand 20 minutes before serving to thicken and develop flavors. Garnish with green onions.

TIP: This dish freezes well.

HUSH PUPPIES

CINNAMON APPLES

MAKES 4 SERVINGS

- ¼ cup (½ stick) butter
- 3 tart red apples such as Gala, Fuji or Honeycrisp (about 1½ pounds total), peeled and cut into ½-inch wedges
- ¼ cup packed brown sugar
- 1 teaspoon ground cinnamon
- ⅛ teaspoon ground nutmeg
- ⅛ teaspoon salt
- 1 tablespoon cornstarch

1. Melt butter in large skillet over medium-high heat. Add apples; cook 8 minutes or until apples are tender, stirring occasionally.

2. Add brown sugar, cinnamon, nutmeg and salt; cook and stir 1 minute or until glazed. Reduce heat to medium-low. Stir in cornstarch until well blended.

3. Remove from heat; let stand 5 minutes for glaze to thicken. Stir again; serve immediately.

VEGETABLES

BROCCOLI AND CAULIFLOWER SALAD

MAKES 8 SERVINGS

1 package (about 12 ounces) bacon, chopped

2 cups mayonnaise

¼ cup sugar

¼ cup white or apple cider vinegar

4 cups chopped raw broccoli

4 cups coarsely chopped raw cauliflower

1½ cups (6 ounces) shredded Cheddar cheese

1 cup chopped red onion

1 cup dried cranberries or raisins (optional)

½ cup sunflower seeds (optional)

Salt and black pepper

1. Cook bacon in large skillet over medium heat until crisp. Remove from skillet with slotted spoon; drain on paper towel-lined plate.

2. Whisk mayonnaise, sugar and vinegar in large bowl. Stir in broccoli, cauliflower, cheese, onion and cranberries, if desired; mix well. Fold in bacon and sunflower seeds, if desired. Season with salt and pepper.

3. Serve immediately or cover and refrigerate until ready to serve.

CRISPY SMASHED POTATOES

MAKES ABOUT 6 SERVINGS

1 tablespoon plus
  ½ teaspoon salt, divided

3 pounds unpeeled small
  red potatoes (2 inches or
  smaller)

4 tablespoons (½ stick)
  butter, melted, divided

¼ teaspoon black pepper

½ cup grated Parmesan
  cheese (optional)

1. Fill large saucepan three-fourths full of water; add 1 tablespoon salt. Bring to a boil over high heat. Add potatoes; boil about 20 minutes or until potatoes are tender when pierced with tip of sharp knife. Drain potatoes; set aside until cool enough to handle.

2. Preheat oven to 450°F. Brush baking sheet with 2 tablespoons butter. Working with one potato at a time, smash with hand or bottom of measuring cup to about ½-inch thickness. Arrange smashed potatoes in single layer on prepared baking sheet. Brush with remaining 2 tablespoons butter; sprinkle with remaining ½ teaspoon salt and pepper.

3. Bake 30 to 40 minutes or until bottoms of potatoes are golden brown. Turn potatoes; bake 10 minutes. Sprinkle with cheese, if desired; bake 5 minutes or until cheese is melted.

MEXICAN-STYLE CORN ON THE COB

MAKES 4 SERVINGS

2 tablespoons mayonnaise

½ teaspoon chili powder

½ teaspoon grated lime peel

4 ears corn, shucked

2 tablespoons grated Parmesan cheese

1. Prepare grill for direct cooking. Combine mayonnaise, chili powder and lime peel in small bowl; set aside.

2. Grill corn over medium-high heat, uncovered, 4 to 6 minutes or until lightly charred, turning three times. Immediately spread mayonnaise mixture over corn. Sprinkle with cheese.

COLESLAW

MAKES 10 SERVINGS

1 medium head green cabbage, shredded

1 medium carrot, shredded

½ cup mayonnaise

½ cup milk

⅓ cup sugar

3 tablespoons lemon juice

1½ tablespoons white vinegar

½ teaspoon salt

⅛ teaspoon black pepper

1. Combine cabbage and carrot in large bowl; mix well.

2. Combine mayonnaise, milk, sugar, lemon juice, vinegar, salt and pepper in medium bowl; whisk until well blended. Add to cabbage mixture; stir until blended.

MEXICAN-STYLE
CORN ON THE COB

ORANGE GLAZED CARROTS

MAKES 6 SERVINGS

- 1 **package (32 ounces) baby carrots**
- 1 **tablespoon packed light brown sugar**
- 1 **tablespoon orange juice**
- 1 **tablespoon melted butter**
- ¼ **teaspoon ground cinnamon**
- ⅛ **teaspoon ground nutmeg**
  Orange peel (optional)

1. Bring 1 inch lightly salted water in 2-quart saucepan to a boil over high heat; add carrots. Return to a boil. Reduce heat to low. Cover; simmer 10 to 12 minutes or until crisp-tender. Drain well; return carrots to saucepan.

2. Stir in brown sugar, orange juice, butter, cinnamon and nutmeg. Heat 3 minutes or until carrots are glazed, stirring occasionally. Garnish with orange peel, if desired.

COLLARD GREENS

MAKES 10 SERVINGS

- 4 **bunches collard greens, stemmed, washed and torn into bite-size pieces**
- 2 **cups water**
- ½ **medium red bell pepper, cut into strips**
- ⅓ **medium green bell pepper, cut into strips**
- ¼ **cup olive oil**
- ¼ **teaspoon salt**
- ¼ **teaspoon black pepper**

Place collard greens, water, bell peppers, oil, salt and black pepper in large saucepan; bring to a boil. Reduce heat to low. Simmer, 1 to 1½ hours or until tender.

ORANGE GLAZED CARROTS

HEARTY HASH BROWN CASSEROLE

MAKES ABOUT 16 SERVINGS

2 **cups sour cream**

2 **cups (8 ounces) shredded Colby cheese, divided**

1 **can (10¾ ounces) cream of chicken soup**

½ **cup (1 stick) butter, melted**

1 **small onion, finely chopped**

¾ **teaspoon salt**

½ **teaspoon black pepper**

1 **package (30 ounces) frozen shredded hash brown potatoes, thawed**

1. Preheat oven to 375°F. Spray 13×9-inch baking dish with nonstick cooking spray.

2. Combine sour cream, 1½ cups cheese, soup, butter, onion, salt and pepper in large bowl; mix well. Add potatoes; stir until well blended. Spread mixture in prepared baking dish. (Do not pack down.) Sprinkle with remaining ½ cup cheese.

3. Bake 45 minutes or until cheese is melted and top of casserole is beginning to brown.

FIESTA CORN SALAD

MAKES 4 TO 6 SERVINGS

5 **large ears fresh corn**

Fiesta Dressing (recipe follows)

1½ **cups shredded red cabbage**

1 **large tomato, chopped**

1 **medium green bell pepper, seeded and chopped**

5 **slices bacon, cooked and crumbled**

1 **cup coarsely crushed tortilla chips**

1 **cup (4 ounces) shredded Cheddar cheese**

1. Remove husks and silk from corn. Place in boiling water; cover. Cook 6 minutes or until tender; drain. Cool.

2. Meanwhile prepare Fiesta Dressing.

3. Cut corn from cob using sharp knife. Combine corn, cabbage, tomato and bell pepper in large bowl. Pour dressing over vegetables; mix lightly. Cover; refrigerate.

4. Stir in bacon just before serving. Spoon salad into large bowl; sprinkle with chips and cheese.

FIESTA DRESSING

MAKES 1 CUP

1 **cup plain yogurt**

3 **tablespoons minced onion**

1½ **tablespoons fresh lime juice**

1 **clove garlic, minced**

1 **teaspoon ground cumin**

1 **teaspoon chili powder**

¼ **teaspoon salt**

Combine yogurt, onion, lime juice, garlic, cumin, chili powder and salt in small bowl; mix well.

SWEET POTATO AND APPLE CASSEROLE

MAKES 9 SERVINGS

1 cup all-purpose flour

¾ cup (1½ sticks) butter, melted, divided

½ cup packed brown sugar

½ teaspoon salt

½ teaspoon ground cinnamon

¼ teaspoon ground nutmeg or mace

¼ teaspoon ground cardamom

2 pounds sweet potatoes, peeled, halved lengthwise and thinly sliced

2 Granny Smith apples, peeled, cored, halved lengthwise and thinly sliced

1. Preheat oven to 375°F. Spray 2-quart baking dish with nonstick cooking spray.

2. Combine flour, ½ cup butter, brown sugar, ½ teaspoon salt, cinnamon, nutmeg and cardamom in medium bowl until well blended.

3. Arrange sweet potatoes and apples in prepared baking dish. Drizzle with remaining ¼ cup butter; season lightly with additional salt. Crumble topping over sweet potatoes and apples.

4. Bake 35 to 40 minutes or until topping is brown and potatoes and apples are tender.

STEAKHOUSE CREAMED SPINACH

MAKES 4 SERVINGS

1 **pound baby spinach**

½ **cup (1 stick) butter**

2 **tablespoons finely chopped onion**

¼ **cup all-purpose flour**

2 **cups whole milk**

1 **bay leaf**

½ **teaspoon salt**

   Pinch ground nutmeg

   Pinch ground red pepper

   Black pepper

1. Heat medium saucepan of water to a boil over high heat. Add spinach; cook 1 minute. Drain and remove to bowl of ice water to stop cooking. Squeeze spinach dry; coarsely chop. Wipe out saucepan with paper towel.

2. Melt butter in same saucepan over medium heat. Add onion; cook and stir 2 minutes or until softened. Add flour; cook and stir 2 to 3 minutes or until slightly golden. Slowly add milk in thin, steady stream, whisking constantly until mixture boils and begins to thicken. Stir in bay leaf, ½ teaspoon salt, nutmeg and red pepper. Reduce heat to low. Cook and stir 5 minutes. Remove and discard bay leaf.

3. Stir in spinach; cook and stir 5 minutes. Season with additional salt and black pepper.

SKILLET SUCCOTASH

MAKES 4 SERVINGS

1 teaspoon canola oil

½ cup diced onion

½ cup diced green bell pepper

½ cup diced celery

½ teaspoon paprika

¾ cup frozen yellow or white corn

¾ cup frozen lima beans

½ cup canned diced tomatoes

1 teaspoon dried parsley flakes *or* 1 tablespoon minced fresh parsley

¼ teaspoon salt

¼ teaspoon black pepper

1. Heat oil in large skillet over medium heat. Add onion, bell pepper and celery; cook and stir 5 minutes or until onion is translucent and bell pepper and celery are crisp-tender. Stir in paprika.

2. Add corn, lima beans and tomatoes. Reduce heat to low. Cover; simmer 20 minutes or until beans are tender. Stir in parsley flakes, salt and black pepper just before serving.

TIP: For additional flavor, add 1 clove minced garlic and 1 bay leaf. Remove and discard bay leaf before serving.

SCALLOPED POTATOES WITH HAM

MAKES ABOUT 6 SERVINGS

- **2 tablespoons unsalted butter**
- **1 tablespoon all-purpose flour**
- **¾ teaspoon salt**
- **¼ teaspoon black pepper**
- **1¼ cups whipping cream**
- **1¼ cups whole milk**
- **2 cups (8 ounces) shredded Swiss cheese, divided**
- **1½ pounds russet potatoes**
- **1 medium onion, cut into thin rings and separated**
- **½ pound sliced or cubed baked ham***

*Ham needs to be cooked to 140°F before using or it will give off too much moisture.

1. Melt butter in medium saucepan over medium heat; whisk in flour, salt and pepper. Cook 1 minute. Gradually whisk in cream and milk. Bring to a boil; remove from heat. Stir in 1½ cups cheese in two or three batches. Set aside.

2. Preheat oven to 350°F. Grease 12×8-inch baking dish.

3. Peel potatoes. Cut into ⅛-inch-thick slices. Layer one third of potato slices, half of onion slices and one third of sauce in baking dish. Top with one third of potato slices, remaining onion, ham, one third of sauce and remaining potato slices and sauce.

4. Cover with foil; bake 50 to 55 minutes or until potatoes are almost tender. Sprinkle with remaining ½ cup cheese. Bake 10 to 15 minutes or until cheese is golden. Let stand 10 minutes before serving.

TIP: If possible, slice potatoes with a mandolin. It produces thinner slices than a food processor slicing disk or a knife. However, the cook time is for slightly thicker potato slices. Russet potatoes are softer when cooked while red potatoes retain some firmness.

DESSERTS

STRAWBERRIES 'N' CREAM COBBLER

MAKES 6 SERVINGS

2 pounds fresh strawberries, hulled and sliced

½ cup strawberry jam

⅔ cup all-purpose flour

⅓ cup sugar

1 teaspoon baking powder

¼ teaspoon salt

2 tablespoons cold butter

¼ cup milk

6 tablespoons whipping cream or melted vanilla ice cream

1. Preheat oven to 375°F. Spray six 8-ounce ramekins or custard cups with nonstick cooking spray.

2. Combine strawberries and jam in large skillet; cook over medium heat 20 minutes or until thickened and reduced, stirring occasionally.

3. Meanwhile, combine flour, sugar, baking powder and salt in medium bowl; mix well. Cut in butter with pastry blender or two knives until mixture resembles fine crumbs. Stir in milk to make soft dough.

4. Divide strawberry mixture evenly among prepared ramekins. Spoon dough evenly over strawberry mixture, spreading with back of spoon.

5. Bake 20 to 25 minutes or until crust is golden brown. Serve warm; drizzle each cobbler with 1 tablespoon cream.

HERMITS

MAKES ABOUT 4 DOZEN

6 tablespoons (¾ stick) unsalted butter, softened

¼ cup packed dark brown sugar

1 egg

1 package (about 15 ounces) yellow cake mix

⅓ cup molasses

1 teaspoon ground cinnamon

¼ teaspoon baking soda

¾ cup raisins

¾ cup chopped pecans

2 tablespoons plus 1½ teaspoons maple syrup

1 tablespoon butter, melted

¼ teaspoon maple flavoring

¾ cup powdered sugar

1. Preheat oven to 375°F. Line cookie sheets with parchment paper.

2. Beat softened butter and brown sugar in large bowl with electric mixer at medium speed until well blended. Beat in egg. Add cake mix, molasses, cinnamon and baking soda; beat just until blended. Stir in raisins and pecans. Drop dough by rounded tablespoonfuls 1½ inches apart onto prepared cookie sheets.

3. Bake 13 to 15 minutes or until set. Cool on cookie sheets 5 minutes. Remove to wire racks; cool completely.

4. Combine maple syrup, melted butter and maple flavoring in medium bowl. Add powdered sugar, ¼ cup at a time, stirring until smooth. Spread glaze over cookies; let stand 30 minutes or until set.

OLD-FASHIONED DEVIL'S FOOD CAKE

MAKES 16 SERVINGS

 6 tablespoons (¾ stick) butter, softened

1½ cups granulated sugar

 3 eggs

1½ teaspoons vanilla

 2 cups cake flour

 ½ cup unsweetened cocoa powder

 2 teaspoons baking powder

 ½ teaspoon baking soda

 ½ teaspoon salt

 1 cup buttermilk*

 Creamy Chocolate Frosting (recipe follows)

*If buttermilk is unavailable, substitute 1 tablespoon vinegar or lemon juice and enough milk to equal 1 cup. Stir; let stand 5 minutes.

1. Preheat oven to 350°F. Grease and flour three 8-inch round cake pans.

2. Beat butter and granulated sugar in large bowl with electric mixer at medium speed until fluffy. Beat in eggs and vanilla.

3. Combine flour, cocoa, baking powder, baking soda and salt in medium bowl. Add to butter mixture alternately with buttermilk, beating well after each addition. Pour batter evenly into prepared pans.

4. Bake 25 to 30 minutes or until toothpick inserted into centers comes out clean. Cool in pans 10 minutes; remove to wire racks to cool completely.

5. Meanwhile, prepare Creamy Chocolate Frosting. Place one cake layer on serving plate; spread with frosting. Repeat with remaining two cake layers and frosting. Frost side and top of cake.

CREAMY CHOCOLATE FROSTING

MAKES ABOUT 2½ CUPS

 6 tablespoons (¾ stick) butter, softened

 5 cups powdered sugar

 ½ cup unsweetened cocoa powder

 6 tablespoons milk

 1 teaspoon vanilla

1. Beat butter in large bowl with electric mixer at medium speed until creamy. Gradually add powdered sugar and cocoa, beating until smooth.

2. Add milk and vanilla; beat until desired consistency is reached.

CLASSIC APPLE PIE

MAKES 8 SERVINGS

PIE CRUST

- 2 **cups all-purpose flour**
- ¼ **teaspoon salt**
- 6 **tablespoons (¾ stick) cold butter**
- 6 **tablespoons shortening**
- 6 **to 8 tablespoons cold water**

PIE FILLING

- 6 **cups sliced Granny Smith, Crispin or other firm-fleshed apples (about 6 medium)**
- ½ **cup sugar**
- 1 **tablespoon cornstarch**
- 2 **teaspoons lemon juice**
- ½ **teaspoon ground cinnamon**
- ½ **teaspoon vanilla**
- ⅛ **teaspoon salt**
- ⅛ **teaspoon ground nutmeg**
- ⅛ **teaspoon ground cloves**
- 1 **egg white, beaten**

1. For Crust, combine flour and ¼ teaspoon salt in medium bowl. Cut in butter and shortening with pastry blender or two knives until mixture resembles coarse crumbs. Sprinkle water, 1 tablespoon at a time, over flour mixture, mixing until dough forms. Divide dough in half. Form each half into a disc; wrap in plastic wrap. Refrigerate 30 minutes.

2. Preheat oven to 350°F. Combine apples, sugar, cornstarch, lemon juice, cinnamon, vanilla, ⅛ teaspoon salt, nutmeg and cloves in large bowl; toss to coat.

3. Coat 9-inch pie plate with nonstick cooking spray. Roll one disc of dough into 12-inch circle on floured surface. Line prepared pie plate. Spoon apple mixture into crust. Roll smaller disc of dough into 10-inch circle. Cut into ½-inch strips. Arrange in lattice design over fruit. Seal and flute edge; brush with egg white.

4. Bake 40 minutes or until crust is golden brown. Cool completely on wire rack.

CANDY BAR ICE CREAM

MAKES ABOUT 1½ QUARTS

2½ cups half-and-half

¾ cup sugar

1 cup whipping cream

2 teaspoons vanilla

1½ cups chopped (½ inch or smaller pieces) candy bars, such as chocolate-covered toffee or peanut butter cups

1. Bring 1 cup half-and-half and sugar to a simmer in medium saucepan over medium heat, stirring often to dissolve sugar. Pour into heatproof medium bowl set in larger bowl of iced water. Stir in remaining 1½ cups half-and-half, cream and vanilla.

2. Let stand until chilled, stirring often, adding more ice as needed, about 1 hour. (Cream mixture can be covered and refrigerated overnight.)

3. Freeze mixture in ice cream maker according to manufacturer's directions until soft. Mix in chopped candy bars.

4. Transfer ice cream to freezer containers. Freeze until firm, at least 2 hours. Scoop and serve. (This ice cream is best served within 24 hours of churning.)

HONEY GINGERSNAPS

MAKES 3½ DOZEN

2 cups all-purpose flour

1 tablespoon ground ginger

2 teaspoons baking soda

⅛ teaspoon salt

⅛ teaspoon ground cloves

½ cup shortening

¼ cup (½ stick) butter, softened

1½ cups sugar, divided

¼ cup honey

1 egg

1 teaspoon vanilla

1. Preheat oven to 350°F. Grease cookie sheets. Combine flour, ginger, baking soda, salt and cloves in medium bowl.

2. Beat shortening and butter in large bowl with electric mixer at medium speed until smooth. Gradually beat in 1 cup sugar until blended; increase speed to high and beat until light and fluffy. Beat in honey, egg and vanilla until fluffy. Gradually stir in flour mixture until blended.

3. Shape dough into 1-inch balls. Place remaining ½ cup sugar in shallow bowl; roll balls in sugar to coat. Place 2 inches apart on prepared cookie sheets.

4. Bake 10 minutes or until golden brown. Let cookies stand on cookie sheets 5 minutes. Remove to wire racks to cool completely. Store in airtight container up to 1 week.

FAVORITE POTLUCK CARROT CAKE

MAKES 12 TO 15 SERVINGS

1 package (about 15 ounces) yellow cake mix

1 package (4-serving size) vanilla instant pudding and pie filling mix

3 cups grated carrots

1 can (8 ounces) crushed pineapple, undrained

4 eggs

½ cup chopped walnuts

½ cup water

2 teaspoons ground cinnamon

2 packages (8 ounces each) cream cheese, softened

½ cup (1 stick) butter, softened

2 teaspoons vanilla

2 cups powdered sugar, sifted

1. Preheat oven to 350°F. Spray 13×9-inch baking dish with nonstick cooking spray.

2. Combine cake mix, pudding mix, carrots, pineapple, eggs, walnuts, water and cinnamon in large bowl. Beat with electric mixer at low speed 30 seconds. Beat at medium speed 2 minutes. Pour batter into prepared baking dish.

3. Bake 40 to 45 minutes or until toothpick inserted into center comes out clean. Cool completely in baking dish on wire rack.

4. Beat cream cheese, butter and vanilla in medium bowl with electric mixer at medium-high speed 2 minutes or until fluffy. Gradually add powdered sugar, beating well after each addition. Spread over top of cake.

CHOCOLATE CHIP SKILLET COOKIE

MAKES 8 SERVINGS

1¾ cups all-purpose flour

1 teaspoon baking soda

1 teaspoon salt

¾ cup (1½ sticks) butter, softened

¾ cup packed brown sugar

½ cup granulated sugar

2 eggs

1 teaspoon vanilla

1 package (12 ounces) semisweet chocolate chips

Sea salt (optional)

Ice cream (optional)

1. Preheat oven to 350°F.

2. Combine flour, baking soda and salt in medium bowl. Beat butter, brown sugar and granulated sugar in large bowl with electric mixer at medium speed until creamy. Beat in eggs and vanilla until well blended. Gradually beat in flour mixture at low speed just until blended. Stir in chocolate chips. Press batter evenly into well-seasoned* large (10-inch) cast iron skillet. Sprinkle lightly with sea salt, if desired.

3. Bake 35 minutes or until top and edges are golden brown but cookie is still soft in center. Cool on wire rack 10 minutes before cutting into wedges. Serve warm with ice cream, if desired.

*If skillet is not well seasoned, brush lightly with melted butter or vegetable oil.

RED VELVET WHOOPIES

MAKES ABOUT 18 WHOOPIE PIES

1¾ cups all-purpose flour

½ teaspoon baking powder

½ teaspoon baking soda

¼ teaspoon salt

2 tablespoons red food coloring

1½ tablespoons unsweetened cocoa powder

1 cup (2 sticks) butter, softened, divided

½ cup granulated sugar

½ cup packed brown sugar

1 egg

2 teaspoons vanilla, divided

⅓ cup buttermilk

2 teaspoons apple cider vinegar

1 package (8 ounces) cream cheese, softened

2½ cups powdered sugar

1. Preheat oven to 350°F. Line three cookie sheets with parchment paper. Combine flour, baking powder, baking soda and salt in medium bowl.

2. Combine food coloring and cocoa in large bowl; whisk until smooth paste is formed. Add ½ cup butter, granulated sugar and brown sugar; beat with electric mixer at medium speed 3 minutes or until smooth and fluffy. Add egg and 1 teaspoon vanilla; beat 1 minute. Add buttermilk and vinegar; beat 1 minute. Add flour mixture; beat at low speed just until combined. Spoon tablespoonfuls of batter onto prepared cookie sheets.

3. Bake 10 minutes or until tops spring back when lightly touched. Cool on cookie sheets 5 minutes; remove to wire racks to cool completely.

4. For filling, beat cream cheese, remaining ½ cup butter and 1 teaspoon vanilla with electric mixer at medium speed until creamy. Add powdered sugar; beat until creamy and spreadable.

5. Pipe or spread filling onto bottoms of half of cookies; top with remaining cookies.

PEACH CHERRY PIE

MAKES 6 TO 7 SERVINGS

1 refrigerated pie crust (half of 14-ounce package)

Streusel Topping (recipe follows)

¾ cup granulated sugar

3 tablespoons quick-cooking tapioca

1 teaspoon grated lemon peel

½ teaspoon ground cinnamon

⅛ teaspoon salt

4 cups peach slices (about 7 medium)

2 cups Bing cherries, pitted

1 tablespoon lemon juice

2 tablespoons butter, cut into small pieces

Vanilla ice cream (optional)

1. Preheat oven to 375°F. Let crust stand at room temperature 15 minutes.

2. Prepare Streusel Topping. Line 9-inch pie plate with crust; flute edge.

3. Combine granulated sugar, tapioca, lemon peel, cinnamon and salt in large bowl. Add peaches, cherries and lemon juice; toss to coat. Spread evenly in crust; dot with butter. Sprinkle with Streusel Topping.

4. Bake 40 minutes or until filling is bubbly. Cool on wire rack 15 minutes. Serve warm or at room temperature with ice cream, if desired.

STREUSEL TOPPING: Combine ¾ cup old-fashioned oats, ⅓ cup all-purpose flour, ⅓ cup packed brown sugar and ¾ teaspoon ground cinnamon in medium bowl. Stir in 4 tablespoons (½ stick) melted unsalted butter until mixture resembles coarse crumbs.

MOTHER'S COCONUT PIE

MAKES 8 SERVINGS

1¼ cups sugar, divided

½ cup self-rising flour

1¼ cups milk

3 eggs, separated

2 tablespoons butter

1 teaspoon vanilla

1¼ cups flaked coconut, divided

1 baked (9-inch) pie crust

1. Preheat oven to 350°F.

2. Combine 1 cup sugar and flour in medium saucepan; mix well. Whisk in milk, egg yolks, butter and vanilla until well blended; cook over medium heat until mixture thickens, whisking constantly. Remove from heat. Stir in 1 cup coconut. Pour into baked crust.

3. Beat egg whites in medium bowl with electric mixer at high speed until foamy. Gradually add remaining ¼ cup sugar, beating until soft peaks form. Spread meringue over filling. Sprinkle with remaining ¼ cup coconut.

4. Bake 10 to 15 minutes or until meringue is golden brown. Cool completely on wire rack.

PLUM RHUBARB CRUMBLE

MAKES 6 TO 8 SERVINGS

1½ **pounds plums, each pitted and cut into 8 wedges (4 cups)**

1½ **pounds rhubarb, cut into ½-inch pieces (5 cups)**

1 **cup granulated sugar**

1 **teaspoon finely grated fresh ginger**

¼ **teaspoon ground nutmeg**

3 **tablespoons cornstarch**

¾ **cup old-fashioned oats**

½ **cup all-purpose flour**

½ **cup packed brown sugar**

½ **cup sliced almonds, toasted***

¼ **teaspoon salt**

½ **cup (1 stick) cold butter, cut into small pieces**

*To toast almonds, spread in single layer on ungreased baking sheet. Bake in preheated 350°F oven 5 minutes or until golden brown, stirring frequently.

1. Combine plums, rhubarb, granulated sugar, ginger and nutmeg in large bowl; toss to coat. Cover and let stand at room temperature 2 hours.

2. Preheat oven to 375°F. Spray 9-inch round or square baking dish with nonstick cooking spray. Line baking sheet with foil.

3. Pour juices from fruit mixture into small saucepan; bring to a boil over medium-high heat. Cook about 12 minutes or until reduced to syrupy consistency, stirring occasionally.* Stir in cornstarch until well blended. Stir mixture into bowl with fruit; pour into prepared baking dish.

4. Combine oats, flour, brown sugar, almonds and salt in medium bowl; mix well. Add butter; mix with fingertips until butter is evenly distributed and mixture is clumpy. Sprinkle evenly over fruit mixture. Place baking dish on prepared baking sheet.

5. Bake 50 minutes or until filling is bubbly and topping is golden brown. Cool 1 hour before serving.

*If fruit is not juicy after 2 hours, liquid will take less time to reduce and will require less cornstarch to thicken.

METRIC CONVERSION CHART

VOLUME MEASUREMENTS (dry)

$1/8$ teaspoon = 0.5 mL
$1/4$ teaspoon = 1 mL
$1/2$ teaspoon = 2 mL
$3/4$ teaspoon = 4 mL
1 teaspoon = 5 mL
1 tablespoon = 15 mL
2 tablespoons = 30 mL
$1/4$ cup = 60 mL
$1/3$ cup = 75 mL
$1/2$ cup = 125 mL
$2/3$ cup = 150 mL
$3/4$ cup = 175 mL
1 cup = 250 mL
2 cups = 1 pint = 500 mL
3 cups = 750 mL
4 cups = 1 quart = 1 L

VOLUME MEASUREMENTS (fluid)

1 fluid ounce (2 tablespoons) = 30 mL
4 fluid ounces ($1/2$ cup) = 125 mL
8 fluid ounces (1 cup) = 250 mL
12 fluid ounces ($1\frac{1}{2}$ cups) = 375 mL
16 fluid ounces (2 cups) = 500 mL

WEIGHTS (mass)

$1/2$ ounce = 15 g
1 ounce = 30 g
3 ounces = 90 g
4 ounces = 120 g
8 ounces = 225 g
10 ounces = 285 g
12 ounces = 360 g
16 ounces = 1 pound = 450 g

DIMENSIONS

$1/16$ inch = 2 mm
$1/8$ inch = 3 mm
$1/4$ inch = 6 mm
$1/2$ inch = 1.5 cm
$3/4$ inch = 2 cm
1 inch = 2.5 cm

OVEN TEMPERATURES

250°F = 120°C
275°F = 140°C
300°F = 150°C
325°F = 160°C
350°F = 180°C
375°F = 190°C
400°F = 200°C
425°F = 220°C
450°F = 230°C

BAKING PAN SIZES

Utensil	Size in Inches/Quarts	Metric Volume	Size in Centimeters
Baking or Cake Pan (square or rectangular)	8×8×2	2 L	20×20×5
	9×9×2	2.5 L	23×23×5
	12×8×2	3 L	30×20×5
	13×9×2	3.5 L	33×23×5
Loaf Pan	8×4×3	1.5 L	20×10×7
	9×5×3	2 L	23×13×7
Round Layer Cake Pan	8×1½	1.2 L	20×4
	9×1½	1.5 L	23×4
Pie Plate	8×1¼	750 mL	20×3
	9×1¼	1 L	23×3
Baking Dish or Casserole	1 quart	1 L	—
	1½ quart	1.5 L	—
	2 quart	2 L	—